I Never Asked, Why Me?

Stories of Gratitude from a Life with Hearing Loss

Enid Denbo Wizig

Dear Margaret —
It was wonderful meeting you
Enjoy the book
With much love,

Enid D. Wzig

2019

Cover Design and Book Layout by Baz Here
Edited by Bambi Here, Lynn Kilroy, and Samantha Morse

ISBN: 978-1986066013

Library of Congress Control Number: 2018914212

BAMBAZ PRESS
548 S Spring Street, Suite 1201
Los Angeles, CA 90013

Contact: bambi@bambazpress.com

PROLOGUE

Many people have asked me – after learning that I was deaf – how I learned to cope with my hearing loss and how I learned to speak so well. Friends and family urged me to write a book about my life and I thought about it for a very long time. I finally decided to start writing in 2004 and wrote on and off with many interruptions.

Now it is 2017, and I have just finished writing.

The reason for writing about my life is that I want my grandchildren to know more about their grandmother and how I learned to cope with my hearing loss. I also wrote it for parents of deaf and hard-of-hearing children so they can let their children know – THEY CAN DO IT!

My mother was determined that I would never view myself as a handicapped person. This book is a testament to that.

DEDICATION

Tillie K. Denbo, my mother, who encouraged me by saying, "You can do it!" She fought for my voice to be heard and for me to be a part of the hearing world.

Melvin M. Denbo, my dad, who always praised me and taught me to help people whenever I could.

Lillian Burns Sidney, a dramatic coach at MGM Studios, who was my dedicated mentor and speech teacher. She always believed that I could "speak like a queen."

Bernard Wizig, my wonderful husband, who was the love of my life.

My wonderful son, Jeffrey D. Wizig, and devoted daughter, Lynn Wizig Kilroy, who had to cope with my hearing loss during their childhood. Lynn has been instrumental in my life, believing in me and helping me in so many ways.

My four wonderful grandchildren: Megan Jo Kilroy, Emily Rose Kilroy, Andrew Scott Wizig, and Sara Joy Wizig. They learned from an early age to make sure I was looking at them when they spoke to me. I love them so dearly.

Dr. Michelle Christie, Founder and Executive Director of the nonprofit organization No Limits for Deaf Children, who has dedicated her life to helping so many children from low-income families. She believes in my ability to do many things (including getting on stage!) and inspires me to keep volunteering to this day.

Carol P. Landsberg, Director of the Oral Education Center, whose dedication to helping the deaf and hard of hearing children be in the hearing world inspired me to volunteer at Echo Center and Echo Horizon School for 29 years.

Jausten Thompson, one of the students from the Oral Education Center, who helped me realize that I was not just a volunteer for hearing impaired students, I was also a role model for them.

Table of Contents

FOREWORD
Dr. Michelle Christie

If you haven't met Enid Denbo Wizig, you should. Within seconds she will make you smile, then wrap you up in her arms and smother you with inspiration. Her endless dedication to sharing her life story makes you want to take the day off of work and hang out with her to hear more and more about her fascinating, heartfelt, and awe-inspiring life. We all benefit from her ability to speak, spearheaded by her mother who was determined to have her deaf daughter mainstreamed in the hearing world back in the 1920's. As a result, we have a force of nature that has unselfishly benefited the lives of everyone she meets.

Enid has dedicated her adult life to helping others. She will talk with parents who are in tears as they have just been told their baby has a hearing loss. Within seconds, you will see parents' fear begin to melt away as hope is now placed in front of them. Enid has served as a role model to thousands of individuals with hearing loss, especially children. Many children with hearing loss often feel isolated and alone, yet when they meet Enid she immediately points to her hearing aids and alleviates their fears that they are the only one. Often, the children will then point to their own hearing devices and a lifetime bond is formed.

As you read Enid's story, you will find yourself wondering how it is possible that she learned how to communicate so well when she did not receive a hearing aid until she was in 5th grade—let alone her first hearing aid being one that was a hand-held box and, later, one that was strapped to her thigh. Even today, teaching a child to speak who is deaf or hard of hearing is an arduous process and takes years of training. Many factors can determine success, including the varying degrees of hearing loss that span from mild to profound. To highlight the difference, a mild loss may prevent a person from hearing birds chirping to a profound loss that prohibits a person from hearing the loud and roaring engine of airplane flying next to him or her. Enid has a profound loss and did not hear a sound until she was 11 years old. She overcame odds that even with today's advancement in hearing technology would be considered remarkable.

As you cozy up with this book and become engulfed in her story, you will be moved to tears as you experience the power and strength of a mother's love for her daughter with hearing loss. Enid shares how her mom fought the Board of Education to keep Enid mainstreamed and made sure she was at the front of the line in PE (physical education) so she could read lips. These anecdotes will make your heart race with vigor as a mom takes on the injustices of labeling a child with the word "can't" and teaching others that her daughter "can." Then to read the stories about how her mom helped her to hear on the phone when a beau requested a date or when she learned how to drive a car, make it impossible not to smile out loud. Her mom's advocacy skills, even when the family did not support her wholeheartedly, taught Enid to not wallow in her deafness but rather to embrace it as a gift to inspire others. And that she did.

Enid's fearless approach to life also made her a modern day legend in the field of animation. You will learn about her job as an assistant animator at Merrie Melodies, Looney Tunes, and Warner Bros, with stories about working with the legendary Chuck Jones. As Enid writes about her 64-year marriage to a hearing man and her endless dedication to her own hearing children and grandchildren, it makes you reflect on your own life and how important it is to live every day to its fullest.

I have had the honor of knowing Enid for the past 22 years. I founded an organization, No Limits for Deaf Children, and she was the one who encouraged me to follow my dream. She is now 95 years old and she always tells me, "You won't let me retire from volunteering." The truth is that I just want her around me every day, so I find things for her to do. Not only do I benefit from her presence, but all of our children and families do as well. The other day, I could hear her from another room. She was talking with a parent of a child with a hearing loss who had just joined our program. Enid was sharing her life story and the mom said, "Oh my goodness, you are so inspiring. You should write a book." Enid laughed, "I did."

Enid has spent the last 10 years writing this book, *I Never Asked, Why Me?, Stories of Gratitude from a Life with Hearing Loss,* for all of you to enjoy. As an educator, this book is a must read for anyone in the field of deafness, but it is also a book for anyone in the field of humanity. She will pull at your heartstrings and give you a boost of motivation, reminding us that we all must live life to its grandest state. The rewards speak for themselves.

When I met Enid Denbo Wizig, it was one of the best days of my life. You may not be able to meet her in person, but when you read her book you will feel like you have known her all your life; a true gift and a bond that we can all share together.

Early Memories:
How I Learned to Cope with Hearing Loss

When I was six months old, I developed whooping cough and pneumonia. My mom was only 21 years old and nursed me back to health. It wasn't clear at the time that this resulted in the loss of my hearing. It wasn't until I was three years old that my parents noticed something was wrong. I wasn't responding to the doorbell, nor did I hear my mother clap her hands behind me. Looking at my baby pictures years later, I noticed that one of them showed me at six months old, holding my hand over my right ear. When I asked my mother about the picture, she told me that I was making the sound, "mmm, mmm, mmm," over and over again. She didn't realize it at the time, but it was probably how I could hear the sound of my own voice. Even though my mother refused to believe I was deaf, she was an intelligent woman and set out to find whatever help she could get for me.

There were no hearing aids available for me to use in 1926, but my mother found a German therapist who gave her a stethoscope with a funnel attached. The therapist told my mother to stimulate my hearing by speaking through the funnel, repeating single words like baby, ball, mama and daddy one hundred times until I was familiar with each one. My mother was also a very determined woman and committed to this sound therapy with me. My parents did not want me to learn sign language. They wanted me to learn to speak orally so I could more easily be part of the hearing world. My mother was always researching ways to help me. She made sure to speak while looking at my face so I could see the movement of her lips. I had surgery to remove my tonsils and she hoped my hearing would be miraculously restored. But these hopes didn't stop her from taking action every day to help me learn to speak and read lips.

When I was five years old I attended Bell School, a public school in Chicago where they had a special class for deaf and hard of hearing students. My mother took me out of the class after only a few days because the teacher was instructing the students in sign language, which horrified my mother. Both my parents really wanted me to speak orally.

In 1929, my mother became pregnant with my brother. She told me, years later, that she had spent a lot of time trying to find somewhere I could learn to speak. She knew that I needed a lot of undivided attention and didn't want to neglect me when she had the baby to take care of. At that time, I was mumbling my words and she was the only person who could understand me.

Finally, she found out about the Central Institute for the Deaf (CID) in St. Louis, Missouri from Mrs. Yawitt whose daughter, Gertrude, was a student there. After meeting me, Mrs. Yawitt told my mother that CID was the school for me to attend. My parents agreed and enrolled me as a boarder. My dad gave up his job in Chicago to move the family, including the housekeeper who would help take care of my baby brother, to St. Louis in 1930. Both my mother and father looked for jobs in St. Louis. It was during the Depression and my dad couldn't find a new job, so my family had to move back to Chicago where my dad was lucky to get his old job back. My mother was reluctant to leave me, but decided it was for the best. I required a lot of attention, learning to speak and lip read, and she needed to spend more time with her baby son. In her heart, my mother felt she was doing the right thing.

There was an uproar among my relatives, who thought it was so terrible to send me away from home at the age of seven. They approached my dad yelling, "What in the world is Tillie doing?" My dad always had faith in my mother and defended her decision. Many years later, the relatives all realized that my parents were right. They saw so much improvement in my ability to speak and read lips and were amazed.

While I was a student at CID, my mother would come by herself one weekend a month to visit me. We'd stay in a hotel overnight and do something fun together. It was a special treat for me. I also remember being in the infirmary with chickenpox and mumps, and my mother visited to make sure I was all right. Yes, she was a very caring mom.

As for my experience at CID, I remember many things about my four years there. There was a small dormitory for the girls and our housemother was Mrs. Cox. The principal, Miss Connery, had a dent on her nose. When one of us saw her walking down the hall, we'd put our finger on the side our nose to warn the others that she was coming. We ate our three meals each day in the dining hall. I hated eating vegetables so much that I would throw them under the table. Whenever I was caught, I would say that the person sitting next to me did it. I was reprimanded many times for lying.

There was a large auditorium that had a piano. I remember putting the side of my face and both my hands on the piano while the teacher played. I could hear the sound with my left ear and I felt the vibration with my hands. She would have us take off our shoes so our bare feet could feel the vibration through the floor. When I felt the music and the rhythm, I would dance all over the room. I loved the sound of music.

I had a wonderful teacher, Mrs. Humphreys, who taught a small class of four boys and one girl (that's me). The boys were Jimmy, John, Albert, and Kenneth. The teacher would take us to the park across from the school where we watched the tadpoles swimming in the pond and saw them grow into baby frogs. We also went to the zoo several times and the zookeeper would put a snake around my neck. I was not afraid then, but now I would be…Yikes!

My friends at school were Marcia, Evelyn, Sylvia, Gertrude, and the twins, Roger and Bob, whose mother, Mrs. Skinner, was a teacher there. What a wonderful memory I have of the playground on the roof of the school, surrounded by a fence that allowed us to see the view from up there. We would roller-skate, ride bicycles, play volleyball, jump rope, play hopscotch and many sports. It was an enclosed playground, so we did not have to worry about the weather.

Even though I was living away from home, my mother wanted me to have a Jewish education. She called some of the other Jewish students' parents and they engaged a Jewish teacher, Mr. Thea. On Sundays, I remember learning about the Bible and God.

I would go home for vacations on the train from St. Louis to Chicago with Gertrude Yawitt, the girl from Chicago whose mother told my family about CID. I always looked forward to going home. During vacations, my mother would take me to see children's plays and ballets. Because I was able to read her lips, she mouthed what the actors were saying or what the plays were about so I would be able to understand. She was a very devoted mother, always helping me understand what was going on in the hearing world.

My brother Donny and I shared a bedroom where we slept on twin beds. Once my brother went crying to our mother, saying that I didn't like him because I wouldn't answer him when he was talking to me. My mother explained to him that I didn't answer him because I couldn't hear well. She explained that he had to face me when he spoke and that I couldn't read his lips in the dark. After that, he would look at my face and open his mouth wide in order for me to understand him.

One aspect of that story is very important: my mother told my brother that I could not hear well. She never mentioned the word deaf. She never wanted me to feel handicapped. She wanted me to feel like I could do anything I wanted to do.

My Parents

My parents were both born in Eastern Europe in the early 1900's. At the time, Poland was under the control of Russia and most Jews lived in small villages called shtetls. My mother was born in Poland near the border of Russia, my father was born in Russia near the border of Poland, and they were brought into the world by the same midwife. The Jewish people were being oppressed by the Russians and many families were leaving to find a better life in America. Though my parents' families didn't know each other, they both moved to Chicago and ended up belonging to the same synagogue. That's where my mother and father met when they were twelve years old.

My parents were both from large families, each with seven children. It was my dad's second oldest brother Jack's dying wish that my parents get married so, at the age of 20, Tillie Keith married Melvin Meyer (Mike) Dembo who was 21. I was born on March 14, 1923 and given the name Enid Joyce Dembo. My middle name was chosen to honor Uncle Jack, and my parents always called me Enid Joyce. Our surname, Dembo, was changed to Denbo when Dad got his passport and noticed that his name was misspelled. Dad thought Denbo suited him better.

My dad was a great left-handed pool player and made money at the pool halls in Chicago. Later on, he had jobs at a liquor store, a deli, and the

Automobile Association of America. Eventually, he found the job he liked—selling insurance. When we moved to Los Angeles, he opened his own insurance agency on La Brea Avenue near 6th Street called the M.M. Denbo Insurance Agency. My dad loved to help people, even strangers. He was the kind of a man who would loan money to someone in need, even when he knew he would never be repaid. When a client needed insurance but couldn't afford it, my dad would accept anything, like paintings, in exchange. That's the kind of person my dad was. I learned a lot from him and am like him in many ways, especially in my love for meeting new people.

When I was thirteen years old, my dad came home one day and saw that I was wearing a pale shade of lipstick. He got upset and said to my mother, "Did you know Enid is wearing lipstick?" My mom said, "So what? She's growing up. You don't want her to be a little girl forever." (By the time I was 11 years old, I was 5'5" tall.) Even though Dad thought I was too young to wear lipstick, he resigned to letting me wear it. I was told that I was the apple of his eye.

In Chicago, my mother worked as the assistant for a blind German professor. Because she grew up speaking Yiddish, she was able to learn some German and she typed up articles for him. Later she worked in a millinery store and would sometimes model the hats. That led her to posing as a photographer's model. In Los Angeles, my mother worked at my dad's insurance agency about three days a week. Once or twice a week she loved playing cards and mahjong with her friends. Pan was her favorite game.

My dad had a brain tumor and passed away in 1966 at the age of 64. My mom passed away in 1996 at the age of 93. I am very fortunate to have had such wonderful parents.

The Early Search for a Remedy

Sometime just before my teens, my mother went to New York to consult an ear specialist to see if he could restore my hearing. It came to nothing. At that time, they could not operate on nerve deafness, which is what I have.

Dr. Brull, a European dermatologist who was treating me for acne, thought he could give me injections to restore my hearing. After several shots my hearing hadn't returned, but he did help clear the acne from my face. Dr. Brull told my mother that he wanted to paint a portrait of me, so I sat for him at his home. He gave the painting of me to my mother, which I now have.

During my teens, my mother even sent me to a Christian Scientist practitioner named Gertrude Sax, believing that Christian Science might help restore my hearing. I also attended Christian Science Sunday School.

Mother was always searching for a miracle. That miracle ultimately came in the form of two hearing aids. Though first, before the technology improved, I only wore one hearing aid in my left ear. This deserves a whole chapter to itself...

On Hearing Aids: How They've Changed

I received my first hearing aid when I was eleven years old. It included a box with a handle that had a microphone, batteries, and a long cord attached to the earmold. It felt like I was carrying a radio.

I was always encouraged to try the latest hearing aid models, which came out about every five years. Before getting new hearing aids, I would have to go to a sound booth to retest the progression of my hearing loss. I hated the changes. The new models would frustrate me at first, but I learned how to use them. The annoying part was how the sound was always different.

My next hearing aid had a microphone that I wore inside my bra with two big, bulky batteries in a cloth bag that was strapped to my thigh. There were two cords attached from the earmold to the microphone, and a cord from the microphone to the batteries. It felt heavy and I had to wear full skirts with sweaters or blouses.

My next hearing aid had a microphone inside. It was smaller and fit inside my bra. The batteries were smaller too, so I could wear them in a cloth bag attached to my bra under my arm. The cords were attached the same way as the previous model. I was then able to wear slacks and blouses, but nothing tight or it would show the bulge on the side. I could wear large sweaters if they did not show the bulge.

After years of wearing batteries on my thigh and under my arm, I finally received a new hearing aid that had both the microphone and the batteries inside it, which I wore in my bra. It was just wonderful because I was able to wear all types of clothes. I was able to go to a formal event and wear a specially made cord hidden in the strand of pearls around my neck, which I would attach to my earmold. That way nobody knew I was wearing a hearing aid.

I could never wear two hearing aids with two microphones because, given how bulky the technology was, there was no room. Finally, in 1975, I tried my first small hearing aids which fit behind each ear. With a hearing aid, my left ear was able to pick up a few words, but my right ear was only able to pick up sounds. When I could only wear one hearing aid, it was always for my left ear. Wearing two hearing aids for the first time, I was able to pick up words right away. It was a miracle that I was able to hear so much better. It opened up a new world for me.

Over the years I've worn hearing aids by Radio Ear, Zenith, Seiman, Phonic, and Phonax. A few years ago, I decided to try the Oticon digital hearing aids. It took me a long time to get used to digital, but I did find that I was able to hear much better than I could with the analog aids. I have had to make so many adjustments over the years, but ultimately it's improved my ability to understand what people are saying.

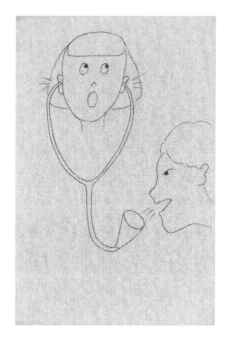

My mother spoke into a stethoscope to stimulate my hearing, repeating words 100 times, 1926

When I began learning to speak, I would feel the vibration of my teacher's voice, 1930

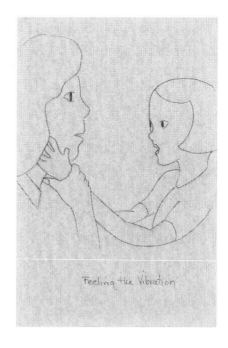

Feeling the Vibration

My first hearing aid had the microphone and batteries inside a box that I carried with me, 1934

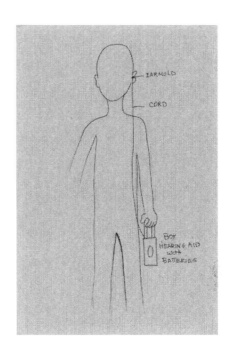

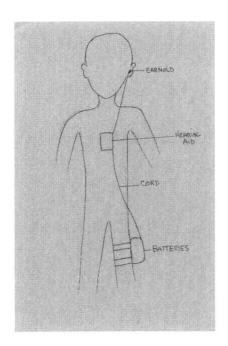

My next hearing aid had a microphone that I wore inside my bra and batteries that I strapped to my leg, 1939

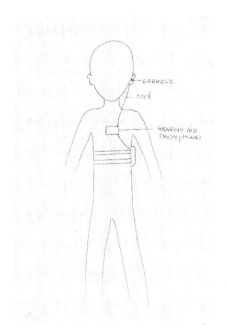

EARMOLD

cord

HEARING AID
(MICROPHONE)

Later, my hearing aid had smaller batteries that I wore under my arm in a cloth bag, attached to my bra, 1944

Ready for Public School

At the age of 11, after attending the Central Institute for the Deaf for four years, Dr. Max Goldstein, the founder of CID, told my parents that I was ready for public school provided I got a hearing aid. So, I returned to Chicago and started at Clinton Elementary School. At the time, my hearing aid was a box that I carried around. When the kids at school asked what the box was, I would tell them, "It's a radio." The funny part was that the device was called the Radio Ear. I carried it everywhere I went and, during class, I put it on my desk so I could hear the teacher. I also made sure to sit up front so I could read the teacher's lips.

I did not stay too long at Clinton Elementary School. My parents put me in the Stickney School, a private school on the north side of Chicago. They had small classes, which was better for me. I remember when the school put on a musical called *Princess Chrysanthemum*, I was cast in the chorus and wore a Japanese costume. But the teacher told me not to use my voice and to just mouth my words. Maybe I wasn't speaking very well at the time or maybe the teacher thought I wouldn't hear the cue to start singing. Who knows? I do know that I felt hurt. I didn't have a choice but to be silent.

In 1935, my parents decided to move to San Francisco where my dad was offered a better job. We were there for six months but my mother did not like the schools, so we moved to Los Angeles where my dad opened up his insurance office. We lived in several apartments over the years: on Mansfield, then Burnside, Detroit Street, Hi Point, and Hayworth. When we were living on Mansfield, my mother enrolled my brother, Donny, in kindergarten at Wilshire Crest Elementary School. She was planning to enroll me at Marymount School but Mrs. Marrin, the sixth grade teacher at Wilshire Crest, said to my mother, "Why don't you let Enid be in my class? I will devote my time to her." She did and also encouraged my artwork as she saw I had potential in drawing. Mrs. Marrin was so wonderful to me and I learned a lot from her.

I then went to John Burroughs (JB) Jr. High School and did very well. I majored in art and had a speech teacher, Miss Butler, who I met with once a week. While attending JB, the Board of Education called my parents and suggested that I transfer to a school where deaf students were taught sign language. My parents were very angry and said, "How do you know what's best for our daughter? You didn't see or talk to her." My parents demanded they contact each teacher at John Burroughs Jr. High to see if I was holding back the other students in any of my classes. The teachers told my parents that they would back us up, and my mother won.

I had three wonderful years at this school where I was the only hearing impaired student. My favorite teachers were Mrs. Beaumont (English), Mr. Corley (Math) and Mrs. Robertson (Art). I always sat in the front of class and depended on my lipreading.

After graduating from JB, I went to Fairfax High School where I made many new friends. They remained friends for many years, though they have all since passed away. While in high school, I did have one disappointment that was quickly resolved, thanks to my mother. One day, I was suddenly transferred from regular gym class to corrective physical education. I couldn't understand why as I had always been very athletic. I was heartbroken and cried to my mother. My mother went to see the gym teacher and demanded to know why I was transferred. The teacher told her that I wasn't paying attention. My mother then asked where I was standing in the gym. The teacher said in the back row, according to the alphabet. "Well then," my mother said, "if you put her in front, she'll be able to read your lips and she'll do well." It was true. You see, I didn't wear my hearing aid in gym class because the girls wore shorts for our uniform. Remember, at this time I wore big batteries for my hearing aid in a cloth bag on my thigh. It was too difficult to wear this contraption with shorts on, so I couldn't hear at all and had to rely solely on lip reading. When I was transferred back and placed in the front of the class, I did so well that I was elected captain of the basketball team. I went on to earn my letters in basketball from the Girls Athletic Association. It felt so good knowing that I had my mother's full support.

All through school I was a "B" average student. I never had problems getting along with teachers and students. They all were wonderful and helpful to me. I never had a special notetaker, captions, or FM system like some students have in school today. Sometimes I would ask one of the students if I could copy some notes if I wasn't able to lipread and write at the same time. I never had problems asking for help. I was always smiling which, I think, had a lot to do with my making friends. I had a good attitude. My five favorite teachers in high school were: Mrs. Moore (Social Studies), Mrs. Mellini (Art), Mrs. Sidell (Science), Miss Heath (English), and Miss Summerhays (Social Studies).

Learning to Speak with the Best

When I was in junior high, my mother was still not satisfied with my speech and wanted to find me a really good speech teacher. We were living on Detroit Street and a neighbor told my mother about a woman named Lillian Burns who she thought might be able to help me. Lillian Burns was working for Republic Pictures at that time as a dramatic coach and later became the head dramatic coach at MGM. She became Lillian Burns Sidney when she married George Sidney, a director of several MGM movies.

It was in 1935 or 1936 when Lillian Burns first came to my home. I was eleven or twelve years old. After our first meeting, she wasn't sure if she could improve my speech. But when she saw my big brown eyes looking at her, she knew she wanted to do everything she could to help. She mentioned that she had never worked with a non-hearing child and that her regular rate was $100 an hour (a huge amount of money at that time). After two lessons, she told my parents that she did not want them to pay her any more money, she just wanted to help me learn to speak correctly. At that time I was mumbling and making a lot of guttural and nasal sounds, so most people could not understand me.

Lillian saw that I was ready to work hard. In my first lesson she saw that my tongue was tight and twisted so she pulled it out so I could learn to stick it out straight. I stuck it in and out fifty times, then up and down. I practiced in front of the mirror constantly and my tongue became more flexible.

She gave me breathing exercises to help me project my voice, including having me lie on my back with books on my stomach. She gave me exercises to loosen my jaw and open my mouth so I wouldn't mumble. During one lesson, Lillian even put marbles in my mouth. I almost swallowed them, just like in the movie Pygmalion with Wendy Hiller or My Fair Lady with Audrey Hepburn.

I also practiced exercises for the vowels – ah, a, ee i, o, u – and later consonant/vowel combinations like rah, ra, ree, ri, ro, ru. These drills were very helpful in correcting errors of pronunciation such as "wery" for "very" and "dis" for "this." I remember practicing sounds like "ha", "p," "t," and "ch," "th," and "s," in front of a candle. I practiced twice a day, five days a week, for five years.

At that time, I had a poor vocabulary because I didn't hear words correctly. Lillian increased my vocabulary by making me find new words in the dictionary and write them in sentences. She also had me recite poems to increase my vocabulary and learn inflection. She did not want me to talk in a monotone. I recited a lot of poems, which Lillian wrote in a special notebook. In addition to the notebook, she gave me the book *First Lessons In Speech Improvement*, by Birmingham and Karp. In the book she wrote:

To my Enid,
May she always do everything as well as I know she can speak, and may
she speak with beauty.
Love,
Aunt Lillian

My mother would drive me to Lillian's home for speech therapy every morning before school, and Lillian would come to my house after work every evening to give me another lesson. That's how devoted both my teacher and my mother were.

Sometimes Lillian would take me to her office at MGM and proudly introduce me to some of the stars that she coached. I met Kathryn Grayson, Debbie Reynolds, Janet Leigh, Dan Dailey Jr., and Walter Pidgeon. I also got to be on the set of the movie *Balalaika* to watch Ilona Massey, a Hungarian actress that Lillian was coaching, film scenes with Nelson Eddy. During a break, Ilona persuaded me to say "csókoij meg," to Nelson Eddy. Not knowing what the words meant, I went up to him and said it. He came toward me with a smile and I, a shy thirteen or fourteen year old, backed away fast. Later, I was sorry I had backed away and did not let Nelson Eddy kiss me, which is what I learned csókoij meg means. (The pronunciation is "choke oy megh" in case you ever want to kiss a Hungarian yourself!)

Lillian had many of the MGM stars autograph pictures to me. My bedroom wall was covered with framed pictures of Kathryn Grayson, Debbie Reynolds, Dan Dailey, Jr., Walter Pidgeon, Basil Rathbone, Nelson Eddy, Ilona Massey, Errol Flynn, Dick Powell and more. Now my daughter, Lynn, has them.

Even though I respected Lillian, developed a close relationship with her and loved meeting the stars at MGM, I wasn't always the most eager student. Lillian was tough and the exercises were a lot of work. I practiced and practiced and practiced, but sometimes I got tired of practicing and my mother would get after me to practice more. I once ran away from home to get out of practicing, but I had nowhere to go so I came back.

As I look back, believe me, it was worth it. I wouldn't be speaking well if I didn't work as hard as I did. I really thank my mother and Lillian for all their time helping me. Lillian was a very dedicated speech teacher and mentor who gave me the skills and confidence to speak in front of an audience. She taught me how to speak "like a queen."

Years later, even when I talked to her on the phone, if I didn't say my "r's" or "s's" right, she would say, "ENID!" I knew right away what she meant, and then I would correct myself. "Good," she would say. She had such a great impact on my life. Lillian passed away in 1998 at the age of 94.

A few days later, Debbie Reynold's secretary called me to ask if I would recite Lillian's favorite poem for the memorial service at Lillian's apartment. When I walked in with Bernard and our son Jeff, Debbie was so happy to see me and called out to everybody, "This is Enid who Lillian taught to speak." In the room were Janet Leigh, Jamie Lee Curtis, Ann Miller, Betty Garrett, and others whose names I can't remember. They were all associated with Lillian at MGM. Before I recited the poem, I looked up and said to myself, "I hope I recite it the way she would have wanted me to."

L'Envoi
by Rudyard Kipling

When Earth's last picture is painted, and the tubes are twisted and dried,
When the oldest colors have faded, and the youngest critic has died,
We shall rest, and faith, we shall need it—lie down for an aeon or two,
Till the Master of all Good Workmen shall set us to work anew!

And those that were good shall be happy: they shall sit in a golden chair;
They shall splash at a ten-league canvas, with brushes of comet's hair;
They shall find real saints to draw from—Magdalene, Peter, and Paul;
They'll work for an age at a sitting and never be tired at all.

And only the Master shall praise us, and only the Master shall blame;
And no one will work for the money, and no one will work for fame;
But each for the joy of the working, and each in his separate star,
Shall draw the Thing as he sees It, for the God of Things as They Are!

It was the first poem she taught me to recite. My son Jeff was so impressed, as he had never heard me recite. Bernard was so proud of me that he had tears in his eyes. Debbie Reynolds told me that "our" Lillian would have been so proud of me and Jamie Lee Curtis put both her hands on my cheeks and said, "That was beautiful." Later, Jamie Lee Curtis gave me a stack of Lillian's books of poems (one of them had the Kipling poem in it) and said that Lillian would want me to have them. I was so touched and have cherished them to this day. As I was getting ready to leave, I noticed a small oil painting of a vase of flowers sitting on the coffee table. It was a painting that I had made for Lillian. As I thanked Jamie Lee again for the books, I gave her the painting.

Lillian once told me that she regarded me as "her daughter" even though I was Mike and Tillie's daughter. I loved and respected her very much. Lillian Burns Sidney was a brilliant woman and teacher, and her lessons are still with me. I continue to practice my exercises whenever I feel the need and I always think of her whenever I give a speech. I still miss her very much.

Dating in my Teenage Years

When I was about 15 or 16 years old, I started to go on dates with the sons or nephews of my parents' friends. The boy's parents would drop him off and my dad (who was very protective of me) would escort us to someone's home for a party or to the movies.

There was one neighborhood boy named Bob Elroy who I liked very much. He would love to eat my mom's homemade cookies whenever he came over. I would go to visit at his home too where he lived with his father, sister, and his sister's husband. They were all so nice. Bob and I would sometimes walk to junior high school together. The day he turned sixteen, he got his driver's license and wanted to take me for a ride in his sister's car. He asked my dad for permission. Dad insisted that he should go along for the ride, sitting in the back to test his driving skills. Bob took us out for a long ride in traffic, down to the beach in Santa Monica to prove what a good driver he was. Dad liked Bob and was very satisfied with his driving.

Bob loved to tease me and it never bothered him that I was hearing impaired. After we graduated from junior high, he went to Los Angeles High School and I went to Fairfax High. We were very good friends for a long time, and we always had good times together. He joined the army (I don't know whether or not he was drafted) in the 1940s. While Bob was in the army, he asked me to draw a logo for his plane. He wanted a picture of a baby in a diaper, wearing a helmet and boots, riding on a bomb like a cowboy. I even sent him a pin up picture of me in shorts, a bandana around my bust, with a white flower on the left side of my head to hide my hearing aid. I had long hair back then. Other fellows in his unit wanted the picture of me, but I didn't send them.

I remember having a date with a navy officer who was in Los Angeles on leave. He was the brother-in-law to my cousin, Janet, from New York. I showed him the town, which pleased him, and he took me out to really nice restaurants for dinner. We dated a few times and he liked me very much. He was so nice, but I was not too keen on him.

Whenever I got a call from a boy asking for a date, my mom (God bless her) would listen on the phone and mouth his words to me so I knew how to answer. Mother knew it wasn't right to do that, but she wanted me to have a date. When my date came to the front door, my mother helped me out again by coming upstairs to my room to tell me if the boy was tall or short. That way I knew which heels to wear – high or low. That was a riot.

When I was old enough to drink, my mother helped me figure out how much I could drink on a date. She sat me down at the table and lined up four shots of bourbon in front of me. I drank the first one and didn't feel a thing. I drank the second one and still didn't feel anything. After the third drink, I felt it. My mother said, "Two's your limit." Now if I drank that much, I'd pass out.

Sometimes I would have blind dates that didn't work out, maybe because some of the fellows were not comfortable with my wearing a hearing aid. Many times I was not comfortable with someone I had gone on a blind date with, so I was fine when they didn't call back. I always had good times with my girlfriends going roller skating, ice skating, seeing movies, playing tennis, bowling and going out for lunches. Sometimes my parents would take me out to see plays, ballets, and operas. I would take my binoculars along so I could read the actors' lips, which I still do if I don't get good seats.

Building Confidence

At the age of eighteen, my mother encouraged me to fly by myself to visit my cousin, Janet, in Amsterdam, New York. My mother had confidence in me to take the trip alone. Janet and I had planned to go to New York City together but, unfortunately, my cousin got sick. My mother insisted that I go alone, so I did and stayed at the Taft Hotel on Times Square. To be out at night alone with so many people around was quite an experience for me.

My audiologist in Los Angeles recommended that I visit Grant's Tomb, so the next day I got on the bus at Fifth Avenue and headed uptown. While riding the bus, I suddenly realized I didn't know who Grant was or why I was going to visit his tomb. I immediately got off the bus and ended up in Harlem Square. I was scared to be in an unfamiliar area, but realized that I wasn't too far from Fifth Avenue so I walked quickly and took another bus to the Metropolitan Museum of Art.

This experience gave me much more confidence in myself and helped me to not feel handicapped. My mother had a lot of courage to let me go alone to a big city. She was so proud of me and knew in her heart that I could be a competent, confident, independent woman.

When I came home to Los Angeles, I found out who Grant was—he was Ulysses S. Grant, the eighteenth President of the United States. I didn't even remember studying him in school.

When I was eighteen years old, my mother said it was time that I learn to drive and that she would teach me. I told her that I didn't want to learn to drive. "Why?" she asked. "I feel like you would worry about me when I went out driving," I answered. My mother promised she would not worry, so I learned to drive and later passed both the written and practical driver's tests. The instructor told my mother that she wouldn't have to worry about my driving; that my being hearing impaired actually made me a better driver because I would use my eyes to concentrate on the road. By then I was thrilled to be driving.

I remember the first time I took the car downtown. I had the radio on because I loved to hear the music. When I stopped at a red signal light, I noticed that some people were shouting and pointing at me. I couldn't make out what was going on until I looked in the rear view mirror and, sure enough, there was a fire truck behind me that I was blocking. I immediately moved over to the side. When I told my dad about it, he told me not to turn the radio on when I was driving alone so that I could hear sirens. I never drove with the radio on again. Years later, if I wanted to use my cell phone in the car, I would pull over to talk. How else could I do it? I need to adjust my hearing aid to use the phone.

I was such a good driver that one day, after I accompanied my dad to San Pedro while he passed out brochures about insurance, Dad asked me to drive home. I drove with confidence and Dad was so proud of me. Then he made me drive on the freeway. That was quite an experience. I thank both my parents for having confidence in their daughter's ability to drive. They always gave me so much encouragement, making me believe, "I can do it."

My First Job: Animation at Merrie Melodies and Looney Tunes

After I graduated from Fairfax High School in 1942, I went to Los Angeles City College because I heard they had a good art department. There I took anatomy, life drawing, perspective drawing and other related subjects. I didn't know why I had to take perspective drawing, but luckily it helped me a great deal in my future job.

I wanted to get a summer job after my first year of college. Gertrude Sax, the Christian Science practitioner who had become my mother's friend, saw the potential in my drawing and asked her friend, Ray Katz, to meet with me. Ray Katz was the brother-in-law of Leon Schlesinger whose studio was the home of Looney Tunes and Merrie Melodies.

When I went for my interview on Van Ness Avenue in Hollywood, I was so nervous. I had never been interviewed before. I thought I'd be meeting with Ray Katz, who was one of Mr. Schlesinger's business managers, but it turned out that Mr. Schlesinger himself interviewed me. He asked if I knew how to do perspective drawings. I said, "yes," and was happy that I was required to take that class. I showed him my profile and that nailed the job. He then introduced me to Johnny Burton, the office manager, who assigned me to the painting and inking department. I had to start from the bottom.

As I walked into the great big room, I noticed that on both sides of the room were rows and rows of desks with girls sitting and painting. Every desk had a gooseneck lamp with shelves behind the lamps. In the middle of the room were two desks for the heads of each department, painting and inking. George Winkler was the head of the painting department and his assistant was Betty Brendon. I was still nervous, but Betty, who took over the tour, was so nice to me. She placed me at a desk between two girls. I took a liking to the girl on my right at once. Her name was Angie and she always helped me when needed. I don't remember her last name, but I do remember attending her Russian Orthodox wedding which was beautiful and very unique.

Cartoons are made up of a series of drawings. Animators do the key drawings that show the overall story. Assistant animators do the breakdowns which are the drawings that show the characters' gestures and emotions. The inbetweeners draw the pictures in between so, on film, the actions look like they flow. For each drawing, the inkers put a clear piece of celluloid (or cel) over the drawing and trace the drawing onto the cel with ink. After the ink dries, the painters are given the cels, along with a model sheet showing what colors to paint the reverse side.

My first job was to paint the cels. On my right hand, I wore a white glove with the fingers cut out so I could hold the paintbrush. On my left hand, I wore a full white glove so I would not to smear the cel while holding it in place. I painted the light colors first, followed by the darker colors. The sheets had to be really dry before adding the next color or the colors would bleed. The shelves behind the gooseneck lamps were where the wet cels were placed to dry before painting the next color. I followed the directions and was pleased to do a good job.

I was very happy working in the studio and made many friends, including Martha Goldman Sigall who later became my best friend. She was one of the legends who wrote the book *Living Life Inside the Lines: Tales from the Golden Age of Animation*. A great book.

While I was working at Schlesinger's, I would get a ride to the studio from Manny Gould who was an animator in Bob Clampett's unit. My mother would wake me up because I couldn't hear the alarm clock ring. My mother got tired of waking me up at 6:30 AM so I could be at work by 8:00 AM, so she trained my wonderful dog Patsy, a mixture of German Shepherd and Collie, to wake me up when the alarm went off. Patsy would use her paw to wake me, but if that didn't work she would use her teeth to pull the blankets off me. That always did the trick. Once I was awake, I'd give her one of the treats that I kept on my nightstand. If I was home alone, Patsy would let me know when someone rang the doorbell. She would run up to my room, then run up and down the stairs, barking, until I followed her to the front door. She was a very smart dog and I loved her so much.

Patsy didn't just help me. I remember when my nine-year-old cousin Ina Sue and her mother, my Aunt Ceil, visited from Chicago. Ina Sue was blind and Patsy would follow her up and down the stairs to protect her from falling. How Patsy sensed that Ina Sue was blind was unbelievable. Patsy was fourteen years old when she died in my mother's arms in the backyard. How we cried. She was the best dog we ever had.

But remembering Patsy has gotten me off track for this chapter, which is about my first job. Well, at the end of the summer, my mother reminded me it was time to go back to college. I told her that I was happy earning money and I did not want to leave my job. She still wanted me to quit, so I compromised and told her that I would take night classes and work during the days. It eventually became too much for me to do both, so I left college and was happy to keep my job.

One of the things I loved about my job was playing ping pong during the lunch break. Did you know that playing ping pong is good for the eyes? After focusing our eyes so closely on the artwork, having our eyes follow the ping pong ball was great exercise. There was a recreation room where some of us would play during lunch. I have to admit that I was a really good player.

It was while playing ping pong that I met Bill Melendez and Art Babbitt. Both were animators from Disney who worked at Schlesinger's while I was there. I'm not sure how they knew that I could draw, but they decided to teach me how to do animation. In animation, each action is made from a series of drawings that are numbered. For homework, they each gave me the odd numbered drawings in an action sequence and I would practice by drawing even numbered pictures in between. These are the pictures that help the action appear more smooth. The assignments they gave me helped a lot.

One day, Art Babbitt asked me out on a date. When I told the girls in the inking and painting departments, they warned me that he was a 45-year-old divorced man and to be careful because he was a "wolf." He was around the same age as my parents, so I didn't know how they would react. When I told my mom that he was divorced and how old he was she said, "So what?!"

When Art came to pick me up for our date, my mom met him at the door. She was very clear with him and told him to "take good care of her daughter." I had a wonderful time on the date. We went out to dinner and, afterwards, he asked if I would like to go to his apartment to see his etchings. Not understanding that this was a line that a "wolf" might use on a younger woman, I answered "yes." His apartment was in the Hollywood Hills and had a beautiful view of the city. I don't remember if he showed me any etchings, but I remember that I enjoyed our conversation.

The next day at work, the girls were anxious to hear about the date. I told them that he was so nice to me and that nothing happened. They couldn't believe it. I think it's because he met my mom. We never did have another date, which was fine with me. Art was a very talented animator and I felt honored to have been asked out on a date by him.

It was 1943 and some of the men who worked as inbetweeners and assistant animators were going off to fight in World War II. The studio needed people to replace them, so I figured out that this was why Bill Melendez and Art Babbitt had trained me. After being in the painting department for only nine months, I became one of the replacements in Chuck Jones' unit along with the Wood Twins, Madilyn and Marilyn. The animators in the unit were Benny Washam, Ken Harris and Lloyd Vaughn.

The Wood twins and I became fast friends. We spent so much time together at the studio that everyone referred to us as the "threesome." They always wore matching clothes and lived together until they each got married. Marilyn and Madilyn were very creative and talented and I would go to them when I needed extra help. They also designed their own cards for the holidays which I still have in my collection.

I started working in Chuck's unit as an inbetweener before doing breakdowns as an assistant animator. In my eyes, Chuck was a big man. He was very important, and I was very shy. He was also a great teacher and conducted several art classes after work. He worked with us on drawing contours and gestures. He did not want us to just draw, he wanted us to draw with feeling. Chuck really cared about us and I felt lucky to have been

ANIMATION INSTRUCTIONS

ANATOMY:

1 .. Analyze the anatomy of your character.
     Consider his weight, shape, dress, personality,
     sex, age, physical deficiencies, and also his
     character and philosophy.

2 .. Try to discover the simplest basic form in an
     object in order to handle it simply.

3 .. Make the line of action simple, forceful, and
     dramatic.

4 .. Draw him in proper relation to the background -
     perspective and size.

5 .. Visualize the contour of the surfaces touching
     the ground.

6 .. Do not let the ear, eyes, nose, eyebrows, cheeks
     etc, float on the head.

7 .. Do not let hats animate unless motivated.

8 .. Moustaches as a rule are hooked on directly
     beneath the nose, so make the moustache action
     pivot from that point.

9 .. Eyeballs should work together except for screwy
     effects.

10 .. Keep hands crisp, get character and acting into
      them. Make them dramatic and strong. Don't
      let hands get puffy and fat.

ACTION:

1 .. THINK WHILE YOU ANIMATE.

2 .. CARICATURE YOUR ACTION IN THE DIRECTION IT
     TENDS TO GO.

3 .. Remember that a loose action does not necessarily
     indicate a good action. Practice restraint and
     above everything ACCENT ALL ACTION WITH HESITATES.

4 .. Remember that all good drawing and good action
     have pattern.

5 .. Act out your scenes and try to really BE the
     character you are endeavoring to animate.
     Try to get the one basic motive in a pose or
     action, sublimate minor elements in order to
     give importance to your main action. Remember
     that the core of the action is the important
     thing.

ACTION: (Cont.)

6 .. Get follow through, not only in your action,
but between characters as well.

7 .. Try to get informal, natural supporting action,
and point supporting characters toward your
main action.

8 .. The action of a character is greatly influenced
by its anatomy, and analysis of this anatomy
will greatly simplify your animation.

9 .. Rough your animation out straight ahead as much
as possible. Use rough extremes as guide posts.

10 .. Do not use holds any oftener than absolutely
necessary and then go into and out of them
very slowly. Never freeze a character all at
once.

11 .. There has never been an action where all parts
of the body moved uniformly. OVERLAP YOUR ACTION —
have one part of the body preparing to do one
thing, while another is finishing up something
else.

12 .. Make arm and hand motions mean something. Ad lib
waving is far worse than no movement at all.

13 .. Plant the scope of extremely fast action with
anticipation and cushioned result pictures. Do
not use twos on the inside of this type of action.

14 .. REMEMBER GRAVITY. Any still weight will fall
unless propped up or counter-balanced. Make the
feeling of weight sincere by proper balance.
When moving the foot of a standing character,
shift the weight to the other leg to enable the
foot to have freedom of movement.

15 .. Remember that all inanimate objects are secondary
and react to primary, animate forces. Remember,
too, that these objects CANNOT move themselves.
Give them inertia and give them momentum. THEY
MUST BE STARTED AND STOPPED BY AN OUTSIDE FORCE.
Give them resistance and make your character
strain when moving them.

ACTION: (Cont.)

16 .. The force of an action must be spent somehow, either by slowing down or by collision with some object which absorbs its force. In this case there is generally a recoil of some sort. The general rule here is, that for every action there must be a reaction.

17 .. Temper your takes to correspond to the seriousness of the situation. Do not over take. Do not remain in extreme stretch positions more than two frames. Animate clothing to emphasize takes. Hold down small takes in order to sell strong situations. Make the start of all takes fast.

18 .. Animate your scenes to the proper perspective.

19 .. Animate pan perspective action on long cells.

20 .. Use telephone pole theory to determine timing in perspective action.

21 .. Project circular perspective action to get proper positions.

22 .. Weight, height, age, sex, dress and mental attitude are a few of the factors that influence a walk or a run.

23 .. Approach every run and walk as though it were an entirely new problem. Take nothing for granted.

24 .. A walk going up or down stairs is completely different than one on the level, and must be approached from an entirely different angle.

25 .. On slow or heavy walks, get a maximum of twist and cant to shoulders and hips. This will decrease as the speed increases.

26 .. Keep feet well apart on heavy characters.

27 .. Accent stiffness for age or awkwardness.

28 .. Keep small, cute characters slightly pigeontoed.

29 .. As the general rule, keep palms of hands parallel to sides when walking.

DIALOGUE: 1 .. When drawing a dialogue scene, think in terms
                   of words and word shapes and <u>not</u> of letters.
                   Spend very little time on consonants - they
                   are the accent points of animation.

             2 .. Hold down your mouth animation unless great
                   emphasis is needed, such as singing or shouting.

             3 .. Remember that the upper teeth do not animate
                   and that the lower jaw's action is primarily
                   up and down with a slight lateral motion.

             4 .. Remember that the jaws and teeth are <u>NOT RUBBER</u>
                   and that the tongue is hooked on at the back
                   of the lower jaw, not stuck in the throat.

             5 .. Tilt and turn the head of ____ - order to get
                   emphasis and roundness.

FABRICS: 1 .. Analyze your fabric, try to make true
             #   character of it - its ____

             2 .. Look for high points and ____ the
                   cloth, and drape your material
                   Stress lines will run from ____ of
                   pull to these points.

             3 .. Follow the curve of the solid ____ when
                   drawing stress lines.

             4 .. Remember that a fold will seldom pass over a
                   seam, and that a flat surface will absorb
                   wrinkles.

             5 .. Watch for surplus areas and make them bulge
                   and sag.

in his unit.

During World War II, the US Government asked the studio to create a series of films for the armed forces featuring Private Snafu. They were training films for the troops that showed what would happen if things weren't done the way they were supposed to. The films were top secret so, in order to work on them, we had to show our birth certificates to prove that we were United States citizens. I asked my mom for mine but she didn't have it, so she called Cook County in Chicago. They said they did not have it either. Then my dad remembered that Denbo was originally spelled with an "m" instead of an "n," so we ordered the birth certificate and I was able to work on the cartoons.

In 1944, Leon Schlesinger sold his studio to Warner Brothers. In 1945, the set decorators union went on strike. Many of the studios made deals with the union, but Warner Brothers was one of the studios that did not. Fights were breaking out on the Warner Brothers lot in Burbank. The animation division was on the Sunset Boulevard lot so we weren't affected, but I think my mother became worried. Even though my mom pushed me to do things, she was also very protective of me. She sent me away to Shreveport, Louisiana to stay with my cousins and her sister until the strike was over. When I came back to work, my friends at the studio asked where I had been. I resented that my mother sent me away.

Working over the light board for eight hours a day was a strain on my eyes. I even had to get prescription glasses to wear while drawing. Not only that, I was not happy with the new studio boss, Edward Selzer, who took over from Leon Schlesinger. Mr. Selzer didn't think I was working fast enough and thought that I was slowing down production. None of the animators, including Chuck, complained about or criticized my work. I was young and naive and thought Mr. Selzer was just being too pushy. Edward Selzer demoted me from breakdown to inbetweening. I didn't mind it as breakdown drawing was harder than inbetweening. But the job continued to be stressful with Mr. Selzer in charge so in 1947, after four and a half years, I left the studio.

Six years later, in 1953, Johnny Burton who was the manager at Warner Bros. Cartoons called and asked me to come back to the painting department. I told him that I would have been delighted to come back, but I was expecting my first baby in a couple months and I couldn't come back to work at that time. After my son Jeffrey was born, Johnny called again and still wanted me back. I told him that I couldn't leave my baby just yet. I never heard from Johnny again, but I felt honored that I was wanted back at the studio.

I was so fortunate to have had the experience of working with these legends of animation. They were not only wonderful to work with, they were wonderful people to know. Along with Chuck Jones, Benny Washam, Ken Harris, Lloyd Vaughn, Marilyn and Madilyn Wood from my unit, I got to know Friz Freleng, Roy Laufenberger, Bob and Charles McKimson, Phil Monroe, Dick Thompson, Abe Levitow, Mike Maltese (writer) and Mel Blanc (voice actor). These people created Bugs Bunny, Porky Pig, Daffy Duck, Elmer Fudd and all the characters of Looney Tunes and Merrie Melodies. I remained dear friends with Martha Goldman Sigall and Leona Garber Hertzberg until they passed away.

On July 14, 1988, I received a letter from the coordinator of the Bugs Bunny Film Festival, inviting us to attend "The Night of Nights" on Friday July 24, 1988. She mentioned in the letter that members of Termite Terrace from 1938-1968 would be reunited at the Alex Theatre in Glendale. She also mentioned that we would be called up to receive an honorary award from Warner Bros., paying tribute to our contribution to animation. Those in attendance that I knew were Chuck Jones, Art Leonardi, Martha Goldman Sigall, Leona Garber Hertzberg and Beverly Gurwitz. They presented each of us with a beautiful plaque. It was a real tribute, especially to us girls who were there to receive it.

Warner Bros.
proudly presents the 24 Carrot Award
to Enid Wizig
in recognition of her outstanding contributions to
Warner Bros. and the animation industry.
We thank you for the laughter and for
years of entertaining the world with
timeless cartoon classics.
July 1988

Volunteering At VACS And The Hollywood Canteen

I started my lifelong love for volunteering during World War II with the Volunteer Army Canteen Service (VACS) and the Hollywood Canteen.

The Hollywood Canteen was located at 1451 Cahuenga Boulevard in Hollywood. It was a club offering food, dancing, and entertainment for servicemen who were on their way overseas. Many movie stars volunteered to wait on tables, work in the kitchen, and entertain. I saw Kay Kyser and his band, Groucho Marx, and Dinah Shore entertain. Dinah Shore's husband, George Montgomery, and Marlene Dietrich worked in the kitchen and would come out to say hello. Bette Davis, who was president of the Hollywood Canteen, also worked in the kitchen and would come out to greet the servicemen. The majority of the visitors were US servicemen, but the canteen was also open to all servicemen of the allied countries as well as women in all branches of service. No officers were allowed in the canteen. The servicemen's ticket for admission was his uniform, and everything at the canteen was free of charge.

I volunteered at the Hollywood Canteen every Friday night. My mother would drop me off and my dad would pick me up. I was one of the hostesses, dancing and chatting with the sailors and soldiers. They were fun evenings, but we were not allowed to make dates with any of the men. Because of my hearing loss, many of the servicemen thought I had an accent and would ask me where I was from. I always told them I was from Chicago and that's just the way I speak. I never told them that I was hearing impaired. I was a very good lipreader by then and I wore scarves around my head to hide my hearing aid.

As a volunteer for the Volunteer Army Canteen Service, I would visit the paraplegics at the Veteran's Hospital. When the wounded men would ask me what country I came from, I would tell them the truth: that I was hard of hearing (remember, my mother never admitted I was deaf) and that I wore a hearing aid. I would tell them about how I overcame difficulties and learned to cope with my hearing loss. I also drew Bugs Bunny for them, which they really liked. I felt good about helping and enjoyed making them smile. I would also visit training camps with other volunteers. We would serve the soldiers beverages and sweets and play games with them like ping pong and pool.

When I was in my 80s, Martha Sigall, Auril Thompson (wife of animator Dick Thompson), Miriam Nelson (wife of dancer Gene Nelson) and I were interviewed by the Solomon Group for a 15-minute documentary about the Hollywood Canteen and Stage Canteen. The documentary is part of the Stage Canteen Experience at the National World War II Museum in New Orleans, Louisiana. When my sister-in-law Barbara Alexander and her husband were visiting the museum, she had no idea I had been interviewed and was so surprised to see me in the film.

My parents, Tillie and Mike, in Chicago, 1930

At six months old, covering my ear to hear my own voice

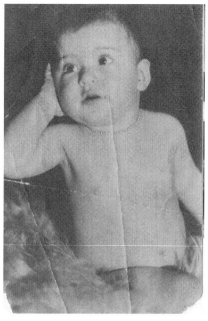

With my mother, Tillie,
in Chicago, 1924

With my dad, Mike, at
Lake Michigan, age 6 or 7

A visit from my mother, Central Institute for the Deaf, 1931

With my classmates and Miss Humphreys at CID, 1931

Proofs from a photo session, age 8

At the age of 15 with my teacher, Lillian Burns Sidney

Sixteen years old

Opening the door
to Termite Terrace,
Schlesinger Studios

Getting well wishes from the animators at
Schlesinger Studios, 1943

A caricature of me holding a ping pong paddle – by one of the artists at Schlesinger/ Warner Bros

Selling War Bonds at Warner Bros with Beverly Monroe, Edward Selzer, Jonny Burton, Rod Scribner, Dick Bickenbach and the Wood Twins, 1944

With Chuck Jones at the Night of Nights, 1988

Just engaged, January, 1949

At Knott's Berry Farm, 1949

Our wedding day, June
12, 1949

Leaving   for   our
honeymoon, June 12,
1949

With Bernard at his 90th birthday party, 2009

Flying with Bernard and Jeff to Waco, Texas, 1955

With my son, Jeff, 2017

With my daughter, Lynn,
in Palm Springs, 1962

With Lynn at the No Limits Gala, 2016

With my granddaughter, Megan, age 4 months

With my grandson, Andrew, age 6

With my beautiful grandchildren,
Sara, Andrew, Megan and Emily (and Gracie!), 2017

Celebrating my birthday at the Echo Center

Celebrating my birthday with Dr. Michelle Christie
and the teens from No Limits

Celebrating my birthday with Dr. Michelle Christie
and her son Jack, Kathy Buckley, and the kids from No Limits

Rehearsing Above and Beyond
at No Limits with Samantha and Eric, 2000

Onstage in "Silent
No More" at the Kirk
Douglas Theatre, 2015

Meeting the Love of my Life on a Blind Date

In April 1946, I flew to Shreveport, Louisiana for my cousin Lolly's wedding. Another one of my cousins, Bessie, tried to fix me up on a blind date with a young man from Waco, Texas named Bernard Wizig. Bernard told my cousin that he was sorry he couldn't take me out as he was going out of town. The next day he saw me walking downtown with my two cousins, Bessie and Janet. I was thin and wore a large straw hat. The next thing Bernard did was call my cousin to let her know that his plans had changed and that he would be happy to take me out. Later on I found out that Bernard had lied about having plans to leave town; he was just through with going on blind dates. After seeing me walking down the street, he changed his mind.

When we met on our date, I told Bernard that I wore a hearing aid and read lips. Guess what he said. "So what? It's like wearing glasses." To me, it was beautiful the way he said it. I'll never forget that first date in a small town. He took me out for dinner at a cafeteria where you help yourself. I saw pumpkin pie, which is my favorite, and eagerly took a slice. I bit into it and said disappointedly, "This doesn't taste like pumpkin pie." Bernard laughed. He knew all along that it was sweet potato pie, but he didn't want to tell me. He had a good sense of humor. Then guess where he took me after dinner. A wrestling match! I knew nothing about wrestling. It was interesting, but I felt bad that the men were hurting each other. After it was over, Bernard told me that the wrestlers were only pretending to hurt each other. They knew who would win. Well after I heard that, I never went to or watched a wrestling match again.

After a week of dating, I flew back to Los Angeles. Bernard wrote me a letter and I didn't answer him. Why? Because I didn't like the idea of a long distance romance and didn't think I would see him again. In the meantime, I was dating another fellow who I had also met on a blind date, this time at my cousin Detes' wedding in Chicago. He also wore a hearing aid and was a radio announcer in Peoria, Illinois. After I left Chicago to come home, he came to see me and we corresponded. Then I did not hear from him for six months. Two and a half years later, Bernard came to Los Angeles in October of 1948 to look me up and we started dating again.

I once asked my mother, "How do you know when it's love?" She said, "I can't tell you, you have to know yourself." After three months, Bernard asked me to marry him, but I couldn't answer him right away. He said, "If you can't give me an answer, then I'll go back to Texas." The thought of him going back to Texas and never seeing him again made my heart drop so fast! "YES!" I said. I felt I had made the right choice. We became engaged in January 1949. The memory of his proposal has stayed in my mind all these years. It was such a wonderful feeling.

Shortly after, the fellow from Illinois called to say that he was in town and wanted to see me. My mother answered the phone and told him that I was engaged. My mom said that he was silent for a moment, so I guess he was in shock. He called back later and told me that he wanted to take me out to lunch to talk. I told Bernard who said that I should go ahead. I made the lunch date, but he never showed up. I am glad I made the right choice.

I wanted to get married in April so I could have a spring wedding. Bernard wanted to wait until June so I would be sure I was making the right choice, so we set the date for June 12th. It would be my first time meeting Bernard's parents who arrived from Waco, Texas a few days before the wedding. Bernard brought them over to my parent's home. When I opened the front door, there was his mother holding a beautiful blue antique bowl that I later found out had been given to her on her wedding day. When she handed it to me I blurted out, "Where in the world did you get Bernard?" His parents were so short. I think his mother wasn't even five feet tall and Bernard was 6'3". His parents laughed so hard and I fell in love with both of them immediately. His father had a great sense of humor and his mother was so sweet. Bernard was the tallest member of his family. Out of the nine children his mother gave birth to, Bernard was also the youngest of the five brothers and one sister who survived.

We had a small, beautiful wedding on June 12, 1949 at Temple Emanuel in Beverly Hills. We were married by Rabbi Bernard Harris. In his wallet, Bernard was still carrying the card with my address and phone number on it that I gave to him back in Shreveport. Before our wedding night, I told Bernard that when it was dark, I would not be able to hear what he was saying to me. "Then we can leave the lights on," was his response. My teacher, Lillian, always said that it was when she heard this story that she fell in love with Bernard too.

Years later, I asked Bernard how he felt about dating a hearing impaired person. He said that when he was first asked if he would take me on a blind date, he did not know that I wore a hearing aid. When he saw me downtown, he liked what he saw. As soon as he met me and learned that I wore a hearing aid and read lips, he was very impressed. After getting to know me for a week, he saw I was a patient person who was willing to work on my speech skills and was always practicing. He thought it was amazing the way I spoke and learned to cope with my hearing loss. He was very inspired by me and felt, even then, that I might be the girl for him. To me, our story is a real fairy tale. My mom and dad were the happiest parents to see their daughter finally married.

We started our honeymoon in Santa Barbara and stayed at the Miramar Hotel for one night. Dad had given us a bottle of champagne that we enjoyed that night. When we drove to Carmel the next morning I asked Bernard, "Do you have the marriage certificate?" He said, "No you have it." I said "No." He stopped the car and we rummaged through our suitcases, but it was not there. We stopped at a phone booth and Bernard called the hotel. Yes, the maid had found it in the wastebasket. We laughed so hard and thought, it must have been the champagne. We picked up the marriage certificate on the way home from Carmel.

When we came home from our honeymoon, I decided to have my mother, dad, brother, and cousin Les Keith, who was still in town after our wedding, over to our apartment for dinner. It was the first dinner I had ever made. I decided to make a pot roast, brown potatoes, vegetables, and salad. For dessert I made Bernard's favorite, blueberry pie. This was my first time preparing these things, so I carefully followed the recipes. The instructions for the pie said, "Season to taste." I never thought it might mean putting sugar on the blueberries, so I seasoned the blueberries with salt and pepper! Oops! So after serving dessert, I asked how the pie was. My mother said, "Why don't you taste it?" God bless my dad, who said that the pie was delicious. Good thing I had ice cream for pie a la mode. It was my first disaster, but a funny one at least.

Another memory of those early days cooking and cleaning was when I developed a rash on my hands. I saw the dermatologist who wrote me a prescription to give to my husband. It said, ""Husband, if you want to save money for the treatment of your wife, please, you wash the dishes."" I was allergic to the detergent and laughed so hard that Bernard had to do the dishes for me. I still have that prescription. I am so grateful for the blind date that turned into 64 years of marriage and a wonderful life together.

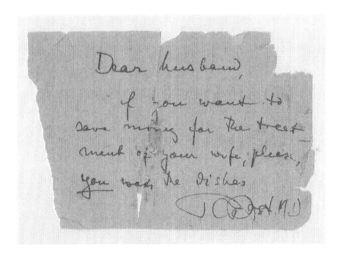

Volunteering at the John Tracy Clinic

I wanted to see if I could help deaf children so, in 1951, I decided to volunteer at the John Tracy Clinic. The clinic was started by Louise Treadwell Tracy, the wife of actor Spencer Tracy, after their son John was diagnosed with nerve deafness. They help deaf children learn to speak and read lips and help parents learn to cope with their child's hearing loss. I met with Ms. Caldwell, Mrs. Tracy's secretary. When she introduced me to Mrs. Tracy, I told her that I was hearing impaired and that I wanted to do what I could to help at the clinic. She said I couldn't help the children directly, but I should go and see Mrs. Harriet Montague, the correspondence secretary, who was also hearing impaired.

Mrs. Montague and I had a nice chat. Her thought was for me to participate in panel discussions for parents of hard of hearing and deaf children. The staff at the John Tracy Clinic would tell parents that the future held many opportunities for deaf people who were well trained. Mrs. Montague felt that if the parents could hear from successful deaf men and women, it would give a tremendous boost to their morale. She spoke with Mrs. Garkie from the Parents' Auxiliary who was enthusiastic about the idea. I agreed to participate and Mrs. Montague and I corresponded a few times before the first panel, which took place in December.

I was excited to see the Skinner twins, Roger and Bob, who I had not seen since I was eleven years old when we attended the Central Institute for the Deaf together. One of the speakers was Dr. James Marsters, a deaf student who was studying at USC to be an orthodontist, gave an excellent speech. He had been John Tracy's roommate when they were both at the Wright School. After graduating, James became the first deaf orthodontist. I met him a few more times over the years and enjoyed getting to know him and his wife. We each gave a five minute talk on our personal background, experience, education, social life, and jobs. Afterwards, the parents were able to ask questions. The evening went very well. In fact, I received a letter from Mrs. Montague saying that I was a big help and a hit, especially with the fathers.

I continued to speak whenever the clinic had a panel for deaf adults to speak to parents. I had the pleasure of meeting Maura Martindale from the John Tracy Clinic who conducted one of the panel discussions with Mona Thalheimer, Ken Levinson and Dr. James Marsters. Mona is a clothing designer and Ken is a CPA who has served on many boards of organizations that support children with hearing loss. I have enjoyed knowing Ken and Mona for many years.

Before I was married, I also belonged to the Valley Helpers for the John Tracy Clinic, a group that raised money for the clinic. I stopped attending after I got married because it was a long drive and I didn't like coming home late.

My Beautiful Children: Jeff and Lynn

In 1953, our son Jeff was born. Our daughter Lynn was born in 1959. Between them, I had a miscarriage. I am very blessed to have my two children. After Lynn was born, my audiologist told me "No more babies," because the births had resulted in more hearing loss. I asked her, "Why didn't you tell me after Jeff was born?" She said that she didn't think I was going to have any more children.

I couldn't wear my hearing aid at night or my ear would swell up, so when Jeff and Lynn were babies and would start crying during the night, Bernard would wake me up with a nudge so I could go take care of them. I guess Bernard didn't feel like getting up as he worked day and night in the insurance business. I did, however, wear my hearing aid to bed when the children were young and Bernard was out of town on business.

It was hard for me to raise children with my hearing loss, but I managed. Whenever the children were crying because something happened, they were fighting, or they needed my attention, I would always tell them to stop crying because I couldn't understand them. I needed them to talk slowly so I could read their lips. I guess it was hard for them to have a hearing impaired mother while they were growing up. But they have grown to be remarkable adults and parents, each with two children, making me a grandmother of four.

Having children gave me more opportunities to volunteer. When they attended Overland Avenue Elementary, I was always helping out at their school. I was a den mother for the Cub Scouts and an assistant troop leader for the Brownies and Girl Scouts. I also bowled for the Overland Avenue School PTA.

Jeff and Lynn had great love for their grandmother, my mom. She would take them to the La Brea Tar Pits in Los Angeles when they were little. They would sit by the stream that ran through the park and call it their Old Mill Stream. She gave them bamboo poles with string tied to the end and they would pretend to fish. She would teach them old songs and make up special stories. Whenever Bernard and I would go out of town, she would have them stay with her. I was lucky to have her help.

She never wanted to be called Grandma and insisted that they call her Grandmother. One day, Jeff was staying at her house and woke up from taking a nap in his playpen. Several times he called out "Grandma," but she wouldn't answer him. He called out "Mom," but she still wouldn't answer. When he called out "Honey," she said her heart melted. When he called out "Mom Honey," she immediately went in to pick him up. The kids always had wonderful times being with their grandmother, and she loved her grandchildren very much.

When Lynn was a teenager, she baby sat for two little girls who lived in our neighborhood named Nancy and Marjorie (who everyone called Margie) Zinner. Margie was two years old and would tantrum when her mother left and whenever she was frustrated. Lynn and her friend Kathy Leib, who also baby sat for the girls, suspected that Margie couldn't hear. They would stand behind her and clap their hands, but Margie wouldn't turn her head. Lynn told me that she wondered if Margie might be deaf. It turned out that Lynn and her friend were right. I didn't know the Zinners at the time, but my neighbor Fritzi Rivin was friends with the girls' mother and told Margie's parents about me. Kim and Ron came to see me to ask what they should do. I told them to go to the John Tracy Clinic, as they do a great job helping young deaf children learn to speak and helping their parents learn to cope with their child's hearing loss. I have loved watching Margie and her sister, Nancy, grow up over the years. Margie wears hearing aids, reads lips, speaks, and also signs. I am so proud of her.

In 1991, I was contacted by someone from UCLA who had a grant to interview people with hearing loss. One question she asked was about how my children reacted to having a hearing impaired mother. I asked my daughter, Lynn, if she resented being raised by a mother with hearing loss. She thought about it and said that, yes, she resented that we would argue and I would turn off my hearing aid in frustration. I felt badly when I heard that. I didn't realize she had a difficult time with me and it was painful to learn how she felt. I asked my son, Jeff, the same question and he replied, "Mom, that is a big and difficult question." He thought some more and said that he, too, had a difficult time with my being hearing impaired while he was growing up.

I wasn't prepared to hear that both my children had resented my hearing loss when they were growing up. I felt hurt and thought about it for a long time. When I told the person who interviewed me, she said, "Don't you also think the fact that they were able to tell you the truth is a very big compliment? They felt free to tell you, knowing that you could accept hearing it, even though it wouldn't be easy." Reflecting on this more, I realized that if my mom was hearing impaired and I wasn't, I'm sure I would feel the same way Lynn and Jeff felt. Both of my children are so proud of my achievements and my refusal to ever limit myself. I love my children very much and have no regrets about what they said to me. I know how much they love me because they show me and tell me and are here for me in so many ways. I am so lucky to have them.

Returning To Work

I was so engrossed with taking care of my children that I didn't think about going back to work until they were older. My thought was to return to animation, but I had not been in contact with anyone for quite some time. The studio where I worked was closed, so I applied at Hanna-Barbera where they made the Tom and Jerry cartoons. The only job they offered me was in the painting department, working the night shift. I wouldn't have minded being in the painting department, but I didn't feel comfortable working the night shift so I turned it down. Bill Melendez had opened his own studio and was animating all the Charlie Brown films, but there was no job for me there. I also had no luck with the DePatie-Freleng studio on Ventura Boulevard in Sherman Oaks where Friz Freleng was working on the Pink Panther cartoons. At that time, I didn't think to call Martha Sigall as we had been out of touch for many years. She was still painting cels, working at home as a freelancer for several of the studios. When we reconnected, she told me that I should have called and she would have gotten me a job. I said to myself, "You can't think of everything." After giving up the job search, I decided to look for more opportunities to volunteer. I have always liked to keep busy and volunteering gives me the good feeling that I have helped others out. I learned this from my dad.

My Grandchildren

When my oldest granddaughter Megan was three months old, Lynn went back to work part time and I would go over to her apartment to take care of the baby. I loved being a grandma and taking care of my first grandchild. I would feed her, read to her, and take her for walks in her stroller.

When Megan was six months old, Lynn told me that she was going back to school full time and asked if I wanted to continue taking care of the baby. As much as I loved taking care of Megan, I told Lynn to find someone else and I would fill in if there was an emergency. I felt like three months was long enough for me. I needed to have a break and wanted to go back to volunteering. For a while I would stop over to make sure Megan was being well taken care of. Fortunately, Yolanda Gomez was the best nanny Lynn could have asked for. She also took care of Emily when she was born and stayed with the family for thirteen years.

As a little girl, Megan loved to stay overnight at my home and help her grandma cook and bake cakes. She loved to lick the cake batter from the spoon and the bowl. Emily also loved to sleepover. She would wake up early and crawl into the middle of her grandma and grandpa's king size bed and wait until we woke up. When I'd open my eyes she would say, "I want Matzo Brie for breakfast." She also loved to play games with us.

I never babysat for my grandson, Andrew, or my granddaughter, Sara, as their family lives in Northern California. But I always loved having Jeff, his wife Deborah, Andrew and Sara stay with us for a few days when they visit. Andrew grew up playing ice hockey and Bernard and I would love to watch him play when we'd go up north to visit. Sara always loved to doodle and draw and has become quite an artist.

My grandchildren learned at a young age that I read lips and they needed to look at me whenever they wanted to tell me something. I'll never forget when Megan wanted to show me something when she was two or three years old. "Grandma, look at me! This is green. Grandma, look at me! This is red." I thought that was so great.

When Andrew started to speak, he would sometimes forget to look at me when he spoke, but I reminded him. Emily was in speech therapy when she was little and got frustrated when I could not understand her. One day she looked at me to tell me something and was so pleased that I was able to understand her. Finally, my youngest granddaughter, Sara, was born. When she started to speak, she was very shy and spoke very softly. Sometimes I would have to ask Sara a few times, "What did you say?" She would get a little frustrated so I added, "Speak a little louder so I can hear you better with my hearing aids." That explanation helped and made things easier for Sara and me to communicate.

Now my four grandchildren are grown, but it still feels wonderful being a grandma. They are a great joy to me and I always look forward to spending time with each of them. Sometimes they let me know they are thinking of me with letters, valentines, birthday cards, drawings, and emails. We even keep in touch by texting.

Volunteering with Hope for Hearing

In 1975, I learned about the Hope for Hearing Foundation at UCLA that supported the Oral Education Center; an elementary school for hearing impaired children. They had a fundraising group called the Woman's Guild and I joined immediately. I remember the time so clearly because I had just gotten my first pair of hearing aids. Every day when Bernard came through the front door after work, he would whistle and say, "I'm home!" The day I got my new hearing aids, I was in the kitchen when Bernard walked through the front door and whistled as usual. What was different that day was that I heard him. I was so excited. "You heard me?!" he asked, surprised. He was so happy and so was I. Having two hearing aids opened up a whole new world for me.

It was soon after that day that I met a woman who was a member of the Women's Guild of Hope for Hearing. She invited me to the guild's luncheon and I became a member. While reading the monthly bulletin one day, I noticed that Jeannette Wachbrit, the newly elected president, had placed an ad looking for a volunteer who knew how to type. I answered the ad right away and became a co-editor and illustrator for the bulletins. I worked alongside Jeannette and her sister, Selma Framson. We became such good friends that they adopted me as their "younger sister." Selma later became president of the organization and I was her vice-president from 1980 to 1982. I co-chaired events with Dottie Shinderman who had joined the organization at the same time that I did. We planned a few lunches at the Oral Education Center, inviting members and friends to see the deaf and hard of hearing students give their oral presentations. Dottie and I also planned fundraising luncheons at hotels and restaurants, along with evening events.

I was a dedicated and ardent worker, willing to give of myself at all times, and eventually became a Life Member. In addition to the newsletter and events, I fundraised by selling holiday greeting cards. I also sewed dolls, stuffed animals and hand puppets, and donated the proceeds from my sales to the Women's Guild. I loved to bake and do art projects, so I could always be counted on to provide cakes for our meetings and centerpieces for our events.

I also helped out at the Hope for Hearing Foundation office, addressing envelopes for mailings to potential donors. I enjoyed working for Millicent Barr who was the director of the foundation at the time. Judy Willey later took over. It was Judy who introduced me to the woman at UCLA who had interviewed me as part of her project on adults with hearing loss. It was wonderful working for Judy as well. Judy left to work as a psychologist and Christine Coleman, who had been the secretary to Dr. Victor Goodhill at UCLA, took over as director. I also enjoyed working for Chris.

Over the years I had the pleasure of meeting many nice volunteers, some who had worked at the foundation for many years. UCLA held an annual luncheon to recognize us. At one of luncheons I ran into Gertrude Yawitt, my old friend from the Central Institute for the Deaf who had chaperoned me on the train to and from Chicago. Such a small world. She remembered me very well and we reminisced about our time at CID.

While volunteering at the foundation, I met a doctor who suggested I look into getting a cochlear implant. I told the doctor that I didn't feel like I needed it. I told him, "I still lipread well and hear with my hearing aids. I'm satisfied." Besides, I was already in my late 60s or early 70s.

In 1982, I was named Woman of the Year by the Women's Guild of Hope for Hearing. The event was held at the Sportsmen's Lodge on Ventura Boulevard in Studio City. Here is what was written up in the next Women's Guild bulletin:

A standing ovation was given to Enid Wizig, Woman of the Year, who was escorted to the dais by her husband, Bernard, who presented her a bouquet of long stemmed roses. Enid also received a beautiful plaque from the Women's Guild. When she spoke about the love and devotion her mother gave her and the training that went into developing Enid's speech, there wasn't a dry eye in the audience.

My mother, my husband, and my brother were there to honor me. My son and daughter couldn't make it. Neither could my mentor, Lillian Burns Sidney, who was out of town. Lillian sent me a letter that was read at the luncheon by the President of the Women's Guild, Selma Framson.

My dear Enid,

Today is your day. And though I am not there in person, my mind and my heart are there with you, your family and all those honoring you for what you rightly deserve.

Well do I remember the first time I saw and heard that half frightened bright eyed, eager little girl and could only say, "With God's help she would one day speak clearly, concisely, and correctly." Her mother was most supportive and helped in the hours of work for five years each morning before my work and her school began and almost every night after dinner.

The first triumphs – when she spoke the full alphabet, each letter clear and perfect – the first time she spoke all the lyrics of our national anthem and even tried to sing them. Her triumph doing the poem "L'Envoi" from her high school stage, her studying the marriage ceremony and saying it as beautifully as I have heard it.

She was the first "non-hearing" or "impaired" child I had ever worked with. She became a part of me – a fulfillment of what I believe: That so-called deaf child whose tongue and vocal equipment are impaired can with the proper training, patience, love, and intelligent parents and family learn to speak first.

My pride in her, is in her giving to the great work that
Hope for Hearing is doing. Her contribution as daughter, wife,
mother, friend, citizen is real giving and my joyful compensation.

I thank God for it – and I pray to God that all the ladies who so
generally give of themselves to help others will know that good in
their lives.

As for you Enid dear, Congratulations and know I love you.

Lillian
Tuesday, 18 Jan, 1983

It was some years after this that a new president, Dorothy Engel, arranged for us to take a tour of the Oral Education Center that the foundation supported. The facility was located on Santa Monica Boulevard at the time. Dorothy's daughter was in public relations with Disneyland and arranged to have some of the characters – Mickey and Minnie Mouse, Goofy, Pluto, Donald Duck and his three nephews – there to entertain the kids. It was very amusing and the kids really enjoyed it.

Volunteering at the Oral Education Center and Echo Horizon School

It was after this visit that I decided to return to the Oral Education Center to see if I could volunteer there. I liked the environment, especially getting to be around the deaf and hard of hearing kids, so I asked the director if there was anything I could do to help. I'll never forget first meeting Carol Proctor, the Director of OEC. She asked if I knew how to take care of plants. I looked at her and said, "Yes." This was a lie, I didn't know anything about plants but if there was an opportunity to help, I never said no. Everything was a new challenge for me. I learned to take care of the plants and tended to them every few days, including when the school was closed for vacation. Later, when Carol asked me if I could type, I said, "Yes," which was acually true. I started typing up the bulletins for her, did some filing, and sorted the books that were donated to the school. One day Carol told me that they needed some help in the art department. I was excited because that was my field. I began drawing and printing for the teachers, doing whatever they needed me to do.

When the school moved to a new location on Venice Boulevard, I followed. I followed them again when the school moved to Sawtelle. I had wonderful relationships with the deaf students. In the first three years (of what would become 29 years of volunteering there), I witnessed an amazing transition in the children. I watched how the teachers worked with each child, letting him or her know that he or she had a voice and could learn to use it properly. I was happy that they did not teach the children to use sign language, because when they speak orally they have a better chance of communicating with people in the hearing world. They can always learn to sign later on if needed.

Every time a new student came to the school, I would say, "I see you wear hearing aids," and then I would show them mine. Their eyes would open wide and they would smile. That's how I connected myself with the students, letting them know that it is okay to wear hearing aids and that it is okay to be deaf. There was a young deaf student named Susan who wouldn't come near me until I showed her that I wore hearing aids. She got so excited that she ran out of the room and brought another student, Jausten Thompson, with her to show him that I wore hearing aids too. He seemed so pleased. The next day I was talking to one of the teachers when Jausten came up to me and said, "Ms. Enid, you wear hearing aids." I said, "Yes." He looked at his teacher and said, "You don't wear hearing aids. That's too bad." I thought that was great. I got to be a role model for the children and let them know they were not alone.

One year, I was asked to spend some extra time with the fifth and sixth grade girls at school. Once a week during lunch, I would throw a "tea party" with Orna Harrosh, Michelle Silvers, and Rebecca Schoor. We discussed many of the problems hearing impaired people face everyday. With my encouragement and guidance, the girls gained confidence. Sometimes the boys, Jausten and Chris Leal, would try to crash our tea party. This was most likely because I always brought treats that I had baked, like cakes or cookies. Maureen Tabbal, an Echo Resource teacher, was also included in many of these tea parties. I loved building special relationships with these students. In fact, I am still in touch with Jausten, Orna and Michelle.

Bernard and I went to Orna's wedding in August 2000. She lives in Israel with her husband and has nine beautiful children (five boys and four girls). We also attended Jausten's wedding in July 2007. I had lunch with Michelle, her mother, Genise, and Carol Landsberg in 2009. It was unbelievable that I hadn't seen Michelle since she graduated from Echo Horizon School, but we have kept in touch by email. In April of 2011, Bernard and I were invited to her wedding. Bernard could not go, so I went with Carol Landsberg. Michelle and her husband, David Berke, were married by a deaf rabbi, Rebecca L. Dubowe, who was once a student of Carol's. Michelle and David, who is also hearing impaired, had a baby boy named Hunter in

November of 2014. Hunter was born hard of hearing. He wears hearing aids, speaks and signs as well.

When Jeff and Lynn were teenagers, they each told me not to expect to be a grandmother as neither planned to get married. You know what I said? "Fine." I felt in my heart that they would get married and have children one day, but in the meantime I had lots of "grandchildren" from my volunteer work.

Over the years, the school has had three different names. First it was called the Oral Education Center, then the Echo Center, and now it is Echo Horizon School. This happened when it merged with Horizon, a mainstream private elementary school. Echo Horizon School is a non-profit elementary school that mainstreams hearing impaired children in kindergarten through sixth grade with hearing students of the same age. This program is an auditory-oral program that teaches the children to listen and speak. One other thing I'd like to mention about Echo Horizon School that I really like—there were no plants for me to take care of there, which was a relief.

The resource teachers at the Echo Horizon School would always ask me if I could draw things for them. I loved the challenge and I never said no. I always said, "Yes," and created many educational materials over the years. Every Valentine's Day, I would hand-make red book markers with drawings of the different Warner Bros. characters: Bugs Bunny, Porky Pig, Daffy Duck and Tweety and give them to each of the Echo students. They were fun to make and the kids loved them.

There was one resource teacher, Judy Kates, with whom I had a wonderful experience. She was very dedicated to her Echo students and would often ask for my help. When we first met, Judy told me that she was so impressed with me as a hearing impaired person that she wanted to interview me. I was impressed with her, too. For a while I didn't want to be interviewed, but I eventually agreed.

Judy submitted the interview to Oticon Inc., a New Jersey based maker of hearing aids, as a nomination for their Focus On People Award which recognizes hearing impaired individuals as positive role models. In April of 1999, out of over 100 nominations, I was selected as the grand-prize winner in the senior category. I received a check for $2,000 and Oticon also made a $1,000 donation in my name to the Echo Foundation. I knew right away what I wanted to do with the check. I bought myself two new hearing aids.

Judy Kates became ill from cancer and passed away on November 21, 2003. She was sorely missed by everyone at school, especially by me. Judy's son, David Kates, wrote a book called *Completing the Circle: A Son's Memoir* about losing his mother. David also interviewed me for a radio piece that he submitted to the Public Radio Exchange. David and I, along with his wife Wynne, have become good friends.

After many years, I felt like I had been at Echo Horizon School longer than any of the teachers. I always loved eating lunch in the teachers' area and getting to know each of them. I never felt out of place. Vicki Ishida, who became the Director of Echo Center in 1996, was the teacher I had known the longest. When I first met her in 1988, she had come to teach at Echo Center as a Deaf and Hard of Hearing teacher. Vicki was always so busy that we didn't have time to grab lunch together, so we'd chat whenever we saw each other in the hallway or in her office. Bernard and I attended Vicki's traditional Japanese wedding on the top floor of Dorothy Chandler Pavilion when she married Mike Yakura in 1991, and I've enjoyed watching their girls grow up from the time they were born.

In 1995, Heather Whitestone became the first deaf person to be crowned Miss America. In May, she came to speak to the students at Echo Horizon School. Heather told her story to the students, sharing that she had lost most of her hearing when she was eighteen months old. She encouraged them to follow their dreams, like she had, despite their obstacles. The Miss America Organization also awarded one of the hearing impaired students, Sheri Dunner, with a scholarship for leadership and achievement. After the presentation, the principal, Paula Dashiell, introduced me to Heather. I told Heather that we had several things in common: we both wear hearing aids, we both lipread, and we both went to the Central Institute for the Deaf. I noticed that Heather was looking at me with some confusion. When I told her that I that was much older than her, she smiled and we hugged each other. Heather's message to the world, like my own, is that anything is possible. My story is also similar to Heather's in that we were both encouraged by our mothers who believed that (in the words of Heather's mother), "Our daughters can lead a normal life in the hearing world with provided training."

Heather's mother, Daphne Gray, wrote a book about her daughter called

Yes, You Can Heather!: The Story of Heather Whitestone, Miss America 1995. In May of 1996, I went to the John Tracy Clinic to hear her speak. I told Daphne about meeting Heather when she spoke to the students at Echo Horizon School and she was very pleased to hear that.

Echo Horizon School was teaching the fifth grade students about deafness and I was asked by the teachers to talk to their students about my hearing loss. I would bring samples of different sized hearing aids that were loaned by the Hope for Hearing Foundation at UCLA. I also brought drawings of the different types of hearing aids and batteries that I wore over the years. I wished my mom and I had saved all the hearing aids that I wore since I was eleven years old. Little did I know they would have come in handy one day for a display. Sometimes the teachers would arrange panel discussions with their hearing impaired students and deaf guests, in which I also participated. It was amazing for me to watch the hearing students ask questions and see them touched by the answers. I always watched the expressions on their faces. Besides talking about hearing loss and hearing aids, I would tell them about my work in animation. The students were thrilled to watch me draw Bugs Bunny and Yosemite Sam on the blackboard.

I loved to see the transition that occurred when hearing impaired students were mainstreamed with hearing students at Echo Horizon School. It was good for the hearing students to interact with the deaf and hard of hearing students. It also helped the hearing impaired students face the future where they would venture into new environments with predominantly hearing people.

As chance would have it, I also got involved in speaking outside of Echo Horizon School after meeting Louise Copeland, a fifth grade teacher at Kenter Canyon School in Brentwood. Bernard and I were having dinner one night at the Souplantation in Brentwood and we happened to sit at a table right across from a long table where several young people and a few older ones were sitting. One of the gentlemen came up to us and asked if he could use one of the extra chairs at our table. I complimented him for having such a beautiful family. He told us that it was actually a group of students and parents from Kenter Canyon School celebrating his wife who had just been chosen as Teacher of the Year. Louise came over to apologize for her husband, Mark, bothering us. I told Louise that he wasn't bothering us and congratulated her. I told her that I was a volunteer at Echo Horizon School. She asked if that was the school where they mainstreamed the hearing impaired students with the hearing students. After I said that it was, Bernard piped up saying that I was hearing impaired myself. Louise then asked, "Oh, could you speak to my fifth grade class? They are studying about deafness." That's how I ended up speaking at Kenter Canyon School three times. I brought my friend Christine Coleman from Hope for Hearing at UCLA with me twice. Christine spoke to the students about ear canals and how hearing devices work. She also brought video tapes showing how loud music can hurt hearing. Although I only spoke at that school for three years, Louise and I have remained good friends.

Service Awards

I have already mentioned several awards that I was honored to receive while volunteering. There are a few more of which I am proud.

In 2000, Bernard was watching California Lottery's "The Big Spin" on television. It had a short segment called Hero in Education, honoring school volunteers. Bernard wrote to the California Lottery and described my 24 years of service at Echo Horizon School. I received a letter from the producer congratulating me for being selected as a Hero in Education. As a part of the honor, I would be featured on the program on Sunday May 21, 2000. I was so nervous to be on TV, but Bernard and my granddaughter, Megan, were in the audience to see me receive it and that made me proud. "The Big Spin" camera crew also filmed me at Echo Horizon doing some drawings and speaking to the fifth grade students.

Another award I received at Echo Horizon in my early years:

ECHO FOUNDATION AWARD
Presented to Enid Wizig
in deep appreciation of her untiring efforts
on behalf of the hearing impaired children of Echo Center.
ECHO FOUNDATION BOARD OF TRUSTEES
MAY 1, 1989

Connie Rubsamen, the Director of Echo Center, submitted an essay about me to the Westwood Village Sertoma Club in 1992 and I was honored for my volunteer work. Bernard was so impressed with the organization that he later became a member himself. The plaque reads:

SERVICE TO MANKIND AWARD
Presented to
Enid Wizig
Westwood Village Sertoma Club
March 19, 1992
For Significant and Meritorious
Service to Mankind

On Saturday evening, April 9, 2005, Echo Horizon School held a fundraiser at Smash Studio in Culver City. The theme was "A Night in Paradise." It was a beautiful affair and there were about 400 people there. They had entertainment and a program during which Principal Paula Dashiell and the Executive Director of Echo Foundation, Norma Roberts, presented gifts to the mothers who volunteered at the school. Then Vicki Ishida, the Director of Echo Center, announced that there was another special person who was being recognized that night; a person who had inspired so many children and was retiring after 29 years. That person turned out to be me! I received a standing ovation and was so touched and overwhelmed. The award reads:

To Enid Wizig,
"When I was very young, most of my childhood heroes wore capes,
flew through the air, or picked up buildings with one arm.
They were spectacular and got a lot of attention.
But as I grew my heroes changed.
So now I can honestly say that
anyone who does anything to help a child is a hero to me."
– Mr. Rogers

Thank you for an amazing and
wonderful 29 years of volunteering.
Words cannot express what your dedication,
hard work and love have meant to us.
You have inspired generations of children to

(in your own words)
"Never give up and never despair."
We love you and will miss you.
The Children, Faculty and Staff of Echo Center

I was so happy that Bernard could be there with me that night as he had just recovered from back surgery.

All the awards I have received are displayed in my home and I am so proud of all these achievements. I'm glad that I've been able to impact so many people with my volunteer work and with my story.

No Limits for Deaf Children

I first met Michelle Christie in 1994 when she became a resource teacher at Echo Horizon School. At that time, the school was being remodeled and classes were moved temporarily to Wilshire Boulevard Temple. My desk was across from Michelle's resource room, so I was able to observe her working with the students. I was very impressed by her way of drawing students out of their shells. For example, I watched how she engaged this one deaf student, John Autry, by asking what he wanted to be when he grew up. She gestured towards a box of occupational hats that she kept in her room. John picked out the fireman's hat and put it on his head. Michelle asked who he was. He tried to say, "fi, fi, fi." Then Michelle said, "Oh, you want to be a fireman," and slowly enunciated the word "fire." Then John said, "Fire. Fireman." He was so happy that Michelle understood him. I stood there watching with tears in my eyes because, before that, he hadn't been able to talk. I thought it was phenomenal how she always found a way to connect with each student.

Michelle told me that she dreamt of opening up a theater group for the deaf and hard of hearing children. She asked if I could finish drawing a logo for what she decided to call the No Limits Theatre Group. I finished the logo and encouraged her to follow her dream. Remember how I shared the memory of being in the musical and the teacher told me just to mouth the words? Well, that experience motivated me to support Michelle. I thought it was very important to put deaf students on the stage and let them use their voices.

While working at Echo Horizon, Michelle launched the first No Limits theater production in Los Angeles. She taught her students to gain the confidence to speak in front of an audience by having them learn four slogans:

CONFIDENCE: I CAN DO IT!
COMMITMENT: I WILL DO IT!
PERSEVERANCE: I WILL DO IT AGAIN AND AGAIN!
SUPPORT GROUP: BE A FRIEND!

Michelle did not have auditions and all the kids that wanted to participate were included. Michelle worked tirelessly, practicing with the kids. It was such a success that everyone was always asking when the next show would be. As a result, Michelle continued to write her own scripts so she could do more plays. I was so inspired by Michelle and No Limits that I knew I had to volunteer. It was very touching to meet the kids and their parents who were desperately in need of hope for their children with hearing loss.

When I retired from volunteering at Echo Horizon, I was in my sixteenth year of volunteering at No Limits. Bernard had just gone through back surgery and I wanted to spend more time with him, but Michelle wouldn't let me retire from No Limits. Michelle was so lucky to have Washington Mutual donate a facility for No Limits on the second floor of one of their buildings in Culver City. When Washington Mutual became Chase, Chase remained a sponsor of the program. Michelle and her volunteers decorated the space so brightly. Each room has its own theme, some with sets and props from past productions. On the front doors of the girls' bathroom is a painting of Tweety in a birdcage with Sylvester, the cat, underneath. The door on the boy's bathroom is a painting of Yosemite Sam swinging his lasso. You guessed it — they were done by me. Visitors always comment on the cheerful atmosphere of the facility and the kids really look forward to coming to No Limits after school.

I especially love being with the kids and helping them during rehearsals for the plays. I also love to sew and have so much fun helping with the costumes. When the kids have rehearsal, I'll sometimes ask if they want me to sit in the audience and listen. During workshops I've even shown them the tongue exercises I did with Lillian and how to project their voices by taking deep breaths. They develop so much confidence in themselves and become amazing actors. How they learn to speak their lines on cue is unbelievable to me. Michelle always has faith that her actors will learn their lines, and she is right.

Michelle started bringing the plays to different states where they have also been successful. Michelle kept following her dreams and expanded No Limits into the No Limits Educational Center. This program allows the children to receive educational enrichment and after-school speech therapy three times a week in individual and group settings at no cost to the families.

The kids attend ten-week sessions and participate in a graduation ceremony after each session. Several times I've been asked to give speeches at these ceremonies. In my speeches I encourage the parents to continue supporting their children, just like my mother always did for me. I remind them that learning to speak is difficult and takes years and years of practice, but it's worth it because, I believe, speech is the most important skill in life. I always end my speech with my favorite saying: "May the children with hearing difficulties be as blessed as I have been when they reach adulthood. Never give up; never despair."

At one of these No Limits graduations, I received an award from the City of Los Angeles that reads:

Certification of Appreciation is hereby presented to
ENID WIZIG, Volunteer
On behalf of the City of Los Angeles and the constituents of the
11th District, I would like to express my sincere appreciation for your
work at No Limits. Thanks to you, the lives of kids with hearing loss
are being enriched as you help them realize the future with no limits.
Presented by BILL ROSENDAHL,
Council Member, 11th District

In addition to helping out at No Limits, Bernard and I made donations whenever we could. In 2002, I started the Enid Wizig Scholarship Fund in a very unexpected way. Bernard and I would enjoy going to Palm Springs a couple of times a year, including one weekend when we stayed at the Spa Hotel. I would always set aside $150 for gambling so if I lost, that would be my limit. I was tired of playing Blackjack, so I decided to try Let it Ride poker. I don't like to bet large amounts, so I went to the five dollar table and watched for a while. When I was ready, I placed my five dollar bet with a one dollar bonus. I won a few games and stopped while I was ahead. The next evening I went back to the same table and Bernard sat with me. I was holding a Ten, Jack, and King of Clubs and showed Bernard my cards. He said there was no way I would win. The fellow sitting next to me quit. When the dealer showed her hand, she had the Queen and Ace of Clubs. Bernard jumped up and said, "Royal Flush!" He was more excited than I was. The dealer said, "You won $25,000." Bernard said, "No, she has a bonus." It turned out that I had won $35,000. I couldn't believe it! After they closed the table, the fellow who had been sitting next to me came back and asked what happened. When I told him, he was so disappointed.

It was midnight when I called Lynn to tell her the news and woke her up. Then I called Jeff. The next morning I heard that Jeff called Lynn and asked, "Has Mom become a gambler?" I told Bernard that I wanted to donate all the money to Echo Horizon School and No Limits, but Bernard was practical and reminded me how I had wanted a new car as mine was twelve years old. I bought a 2002 Gold Camry Toyota LE, which I love and still own. With the money left over, I opened the Enid Wizig Scholarship Fund for both No Limits and the Echo Horizon School and feel so good about donating whenever I can.

No Limits continues to grow and, over the past 21 years, has helped thousands of people across the globe. It's an incredible program that started with only eight kids in 1996.

In the summer of 2000, when I was 77 years old, Michelle Christie came over to my house one day and dropped a script on my lap. "I would love for you to be in the No Limits play, *Above and Beyond,* that was based on your life, you would be so great in it and the kids would love to have you." I immediately replied, "NO WAY!" I didn't think I would be able to memorize my lines, but Bernard said, "I think it would be a wonderful experience for you." Lynn agreed, "That's great, Mom. You should do it." I thought, "Okay, I'll do it for the kids," and I'm so glad that I did.

My first rehearsal of *Above and Beyond* went well, but I definitely needed more practice. That evening, I decided to go for a walk after dinner. On my walk, I tripped and hurt my left foot. The first words out of my mouth were, "Oh no! I can't miss rehearsals! The show must go on!" I put ice on my foot and went to rehearsal the next day, limping with a cane that used to be my dad's. My foot was so swollen that I went to the orthopedist and I found out I had actually broken a bone. I was fitted with a boot cast but, true to my word, I never missed a rehearsal.

It was interesting to rehearse with the children with hearing loss. I loved working with Samantha Dudley and Eric Scargalino who were playing the roles of my grandchildren, Alona Shemza who played my daughter, and David Hawkins who played the Grumpy Grandpa. It was amazing to see the young actors learn their lines and act out their characters. I watched them gain confidence over time and ultimately have the poise to act on stage in front of hundreds of people. Their courage helped me see that I could do it too. Michelle's patience and dedication working with the young actors amazed me. What a director she was! She made me feel so comfortable and always had confidence in me.

All the hard work paid off. We sold out both performances at the Acme Theatre on La Brea Avenue on August 27, 2000. I was told there was not a dry eye in the house. I was so touched by that. After the show, Bernard had tears in his eyes when he gave me a beautiful bouquet of roses.

After the show, I was given an award from the No Limits Theater Group:

NO LIMITS THEATER GROUP
for hearing impaired children proudly presents
ENID WIZIG
with the ABOVE AND BEYOND AWARD
for always going above and beyond
for the children with hearing loss.
NO LIMITS
ABOVE AND BEYOND STAGE DEBUT
AUGUST, 2000

Ten years later, Michelle asked me to be on a panel for "A Night of Remarkable Women" featuring myself and three women: Julie Postance who wrote *Breaking the Sound Barriers: Success Stories by Individuals with Hearing Loss*; Rhianon Elan Gutierrez who is a filmmaker with hearing loss; and America's first deaf comedian, Kathy Buckley. Each of us told about our lives and careers. I spoke about my years working in animation for Merrie Melodies and Looney Tunes.

Kathy Buckley has been a great advocate and fundraiser for No Limits. She supports Michelle and the kids in so many ways, including participating in some of the plays. She makes everyone laugh and is idolized by all the kids and their parents. To me she is an absolutely wonderful person with a great attitude. She wrote a book about her life called *If You Could Hear What I See*. It is an amazing story.

In 2015, I returned to the stage for *Silent NO MORE*, a collection of inspiring life stories by individuals with hearing loss that later debuted at Carnegie Hall. There were eleven of us who performed at the Kirk Douglas Theatre on June 12, 2015. It was a special night for me in more ways than one, which I shared as part of my monologue:

> *"Another momentous time in my life was meeting my husband, Bernard, who I had been married to for 64 years. He passed away over a year ago, but he would have been so proud of me being on stage here tonight. You see, today is our anniversary."*

At the end of the show, Michelle surprised me with a cake to celebrate our anniversary. I was so touched. She loved Bernard and always appreciated how much we meant to each other.

No Limits celebrated its 20th Anniversary at Sony Studios on April 17, 2016. To my surprise I received another award:

> Certificate of Congressional Recognition
> Presented to Enid Wizig on being honored at
> NO LIMITS FOR DEAF CHILDREN
> 20th ANNIVERSARY CELEBRATION
> For supporting the organization's work
> to empower deaf children through theater
> workshops and stage productions which aim to
> build self-expression, social skills and confidence.
> Karen Bass, Member of Congress
> California 37th District – April 17, 2016

Over the years, it has been so wonderful to watch the No Limits kids grow up. I am always happy to see everyone who still visits or helps out at No Limits including John Autry Jr., David Hawkins, Samantha Dudley, Rachel Reiner, Ivy Lee, Jonathan Avina, Christian Reyes, Anthony Magana, and Billy Foran. Many of them are amazed that I continue volunteering there as I am almost 95 years old.

Just this year, Michelle tricked me by asking me to come to No Limits to talk with the teachers about how I learned to speak. When I arrived, she presented me with the Volunteer of the Year Award thanking me for over twenty years of service. What a lovely surprise!

Michelle's son, Jack, is another special person in my life. Bernard and I fell in love with Jack from the time he was born. He became our adopted grandson, calling us Grandma Enid and Grandpa Bernard. Grandpa Bernard told Michelle that her son was one smart little boy. Jack, like my other grandchildren, learned to look at my face when speaking to me. He wanted to learn how to draw cartoons and I gave him a few lessons. I am so happy that he is in my life.

Proud Survivor

I was first diagnosed with breast cancer in 1988. Three of my cousins had mastectomies, so I talked to each of them. They all had positive attitudes and I thought that if they could go through it, so could I. I had a wonderful surgeon who showed me pictures so I could see how I would look after the surgery. I had the surgery in September and was very lucky because the cancer was caught early and I didn't need radiation or chemotherapy. After a week, the surgeon removed the drainage tube and had me look at my chest. After the surgeon left the room and Bernard walked in, I started to cry. I asked Bernard if he wanted to see, and he said, "Sure." Then he told me that he didn't need that breast, he only needed me.

Many years later, I was diagnosed with breast cancer again and had a second mastectomy in September of 2014. Once again, I knew I would be okay. I had wonderful support from my daughter, Lynn, who stayed with me and from Jeff who kept in touch by phone. Michelle was there for me too.

After a wonderful life together, Bernard passed away in 2013 at the age of 95. Even in his last days, every time I walked into his room he would smile and say, "You're beautiful, I love you." This is a poem I wrote about losing him:

LIFE MUST GO ON

After my beloved one passed away—he was the love of my life—
I realized that life must go on!
I lost ten of my dearest friends within a year.
Yes, life must go on!

I just turned 93 years old.
Two days before my birthday, I was using the beautiful
magnifying mirror that I'd had since I got married.
It suddenly slipped through my fingers and fell on my foot.
One side did not crack, but the other side did.

Know what I said?
"I have seven more years to go until I am 100 years old."
Yes, I said, "Life Must Go On!!"

Enid Wizig
March, 2016

So Much to be Grateful For

Back when I was going to John Burroughs Junior High School, I was walking with a fellow student who asked me if I felt handicapped wearing my hearing aid. At that time, I didn't know what the word "handicapped" meant. When I asked my mother, she told me, "Remember you are not handicapped. You can do what other people can do, except you can't hear too well. But you can read lips very well and not many people can do that!" Thanks to my mother's determination, I never let my hearing loss limit my ability to make a difference in my family, the community, or the world. I am grateful to my mother and dad for making the choice for me to learn to speak, and for Lillian who gave me the confidence and skills I needed to be successful.

My mother never used the word deaf. She refused to believe that was my reality. After I had my two children and my audiologist told me that I was profoundly deaf, I told my mother but she refused to believe me. I feel my mother should have told me the truth, but she did not want to admit it. Maybe she thought that if I was deaf, instead of hard of hearing, I wouldn't have had the same opportunities. My mother didn't have places like the John Tracy Clinic and No Limits where parents learn that even when children are deaf, they can still follow their dreams. I'm grateful that my mother did everything she believed would help me to be successful, because she did a great job. I'm also grateful that today, parents of deaf children have the kind of support my mother didn't have.

I am also grateful for the improvements in technology over the years. While I've already mentioned the developments in hearing aids, I would also like to express my gratitude for my wonderful audiologist, Esther R. Daniel. Esther took care of me for years and was the most understanding person I have ever known. I now work with Bonnie Baehr in Beverly Hills. I took a liking to Bonnie who helped me get used to digital hearing aids. Bonnie reads me well and knows what will help me feel comfortable.

Another technology I've grown to really love is the CaptionCall telephone. It takes what people are saying to me over the phone and writes it out so I don't miss a word. Before I had the CaptionCall, I felt frustrated when the people on the other end of the phone had to repeat themselves so many times so I could understand what they were saying. I felt that it was uncomfortable for them to talk to me on the phone. Now I have a phone that works for me and for my callers.

Captions on the television have also made a big difference for me. Before I had captions on the TV screen, I had to read lips while trying to hear what was being said. I didn't always follow the program, but often I could put two-and-two together and figure out what was going on.

When personal computers and email became available, Lynn insisted that it would help me communicate with her and others. It was a godsend. I learned to use the computer quickly and I love keeping in touch with people through email. When Lynn suggested that I learn how to text, I wasn't sure about learning one more thing. When she suggested it would be the easiest way to keep in touch with my grandchildren, I was convinced.

Even with all this technology, I still lipread when having face-to-face conversations, with or without hearing aids. When I was young and out with my mother, she would sometimes ask me what other people were talking about. If I was out to dinner with Bernard and got distracted lip reading other people's conversations, he'd have to remind me to pay attention to him. When we'd watch Dodger games on TV, I'd tell Bernard what the coaches and umpires were saying. Sometimes I like to read lips at the beauty shop while I am under the hair dryer. Once I told my hairdresser, Vera, what another customer had said, not thinking that Vera would say anything to the customer. Vera told me later that the customer told her to tell me to mind my own business.

One day when I was volunteering at the Oral Education Center, Carol Landsberg received a call from Lionsgate Films. They were looking for an expert lip reader to help out with a scene for the movie *Coal Miner's Daughter*, so Carol and I went to the studio. There was film of a square dance scene where they could see the actors talking, but there was no sound. They wanted us to figure out what the actors were saying so they could have the actors record the dialogue. We watched the square dance scene over and over, laughing while we tried to match what the actors might be saying with the movement of their lips. Finally, the sound editor was satisfied. We didn't get paid for our work, but we had a lot of fun and the studio made a donation to OEC. When the movie came out, we went with our husbands and Carol's parents to see it and enjoyed it very much.

While I'm a good lip reader, I don't always catch everything that people say to me. One thing that has always bothered me is when I ask people to repeat what they're telling me and they say, "Never mind." When people do this, it always annoys me because I don't like to feel like an outsider. I always reply, "Don't say 'never mind,' just tell me."

Even though there have been hardships, I've never asked, "Why me?" My mission has always been to send a clear message that hearing loss does not limit a person's ability to lead a full and productive life. I've learned to cope through proper training from teachers, support from family and friends, gratitude for what I have, and by giving to others. I continue to volunteer at No Limits at the age of 94, and am grateful that Michelle still won't let me retire. I love being around all the children with hearing loss. They continue to impact my life, and I impact theirs by letting them know that they are not alone.

When my granddaughters Emily and Sara were much younger, I took them and their moms to lunch at the American Girl store. On the table was a small bowl with questions meant to spark conversation, so we randomly picked one of the questions. "If you could be anyone else for a day, who would you want to be?" We went around the table and each person said who they'd want to spend the day as. When my turn came I answered, "There is no one who I would want to be, except me." It's true. I've lived a wonderful life as a profoundly deaf person and I wouldn't want to change a thing.

Acknowledgements

There are many people who have helped make this book possible.

I first want to thank the key people who helped make the book a reality. My daughter, Lynn Wizig Kilroy, who was determined to have the book ready in time for my 95th birthday. She helped me every step of the way with coordinating the project, editing, choosing pictures, and researching facts to make sure everything was accurate.

I thank my son, Jeff Wizig, for working with Lynn in many ways including editing, remembering stories to include, and working with our wonderful publishing team. I am so grateful to my children for always being there for me.

The third key person I want to thank is Michelle Christie. Michelle is like a daughter to me, encouraging and supporting me in so many ways. Michelle saw that this book could offer some history about growing up with hearing loss and how the supports available have changed over the years. She was the first person to read and organize all my stories. I also thank Michelle for not letting me retire from No Limits. She and the kids keep me young.

I thank Samantha Morse, a graduate student and teaching assistant in the English department at UCLA, who did a wonderful job editing the book over the summer. Sam is a good friend of my granddaughter, Megan, and I've enjoyed getting to know her.

Thanks also go out to Jerry Beck, who I've known for many years through my late, dear friend, Martha Sigall. Jerry is an American animation historian who encouraged me to tell my stories from the early days of animation, including the stories I wasn't so sure I should share. I also thank Jerry for reviewing all the stories from my years in animation to make sure they were historically accurate.

Before I thank my wonderful publishing team, I must thank my neighbor and friend, Roz Levine, for telling Lynn about BamBaz publishing. Roz proves the concept that good people find good people, and Roz, Bambi and Baz are all really good people. From the moment I met Bambi Here and Baz Here of BamBaz publishing in downtown Los Angeles, I fell in love with them. Bambi is an excellent editor and Baz designed a beautiful book. He took my idea for the cover and brought it to life in such a unique way. He is also a wonderful photographer and made me feel so comfortable during the photo shoot. Together, they did a magnificent job.

I am also grateful to the many people who encouraged me to write my book including my beloved husband, Bernard. He read the first few chapters and told me to, "Go for it," but passed away before I could finish the book. I thank him for always believing in me. I'm also grateful to my late friend Martha Sigall for inspiring me through her own book about the animation industry and for encouraging me to write a book of my own. I also want to thank Claire Lockhart from the Academy of Motion Picture Arts and Sciences. Like Jerry Beck, Claire is a wonderful friend who I met through Martha Sigall. Claire often said, "You must write a book about yourself and the wonderful stories you have told me. It would be so wonderful for people to know about you and what you have done." Claire also included me in the Academy's recent panel, An Invisible History: Trailblazing Women of Animation hosted by author and historian Mindy Johnson. Claire, Jerry and Mindy, along with Bambi and Baz are helping me write new chapter in my life, making me feel like life can begin again, even at 95!

And to all those who have patiently waited to read my book, thank you for your patience.